PITMAN'S COMMON COMMODITIES
AND INDUSTRIES

CLOCKS AND WATCHES

BY

GEORGE L. OVERTON

ASSOCIATE OF THE ROYAL COLLEGE OF
SCIENCE, LONDON; FELLOW OF THE
BRITISH HOROLOGICAL INSTITUTE

Copyright © 2013 Read Books Ltd.
This book is copyright and may not be
reproduced or copied in any way without
the express permission of the publisher in writing

British Library Cataloguing-in-Publication Data
A catalogue record for this book is available from the
British Library

A History of Clocks and Watches

Horology (from the Latin, Horologium) is the science of measuring time. Clocks, watches, clockwork, sundials, clepsydras, timers, time recorders, marine chronometers and atomic clocks are all examples of instruments used to measure time. In current usage, horology refers mainly to the study of mechanical timekeeping devices, whilst chronometry more broadly included electronic devices that have largely supplanted mechanical clocks for accuracy and precision in timekeeping. Horology itself has an incredibly long history and there are many museums and several specialised libraries devoted to the subject. Perhaps the most famous is the *Royal Greenwich Observatory*, also the source of the Prime Meridian (longitude 0° 0' 0"), and the home of the first marine timekeepers accurate enough to determine longitude.

The word 'clock' is derived from the Celtic words *clagan* and *clocca* meaning 'bell'. A silent instrument missing such a mechanism has traditionally been known as a timepiece, although today the words have become interchangeable. The clock is one of the oldest human interventions, meeting the need to consistently measure intervals of time shorter than the natural units: the day, the lunar month and the year. The current sexagesimal system of time measurement dates to approximately 2000 BC in Sumer. The Ancient Egyptians divided the day into two twelve-hour periods and used large obelisks to track the movement of the sun. They also developed water clocks, which had also been employed frequently by the Ancient Greeks, who called them 'clepsydrae'. The Shang Dynasty is also believed to have used the outflow water clock around the same time.

The first mechanical clocks, employing the verge escapement mechanism (the mechanism that controls the rate of a clock by advancing the gear train at regular intervals or 'ticks') with a foliot or balance wheel timekeeper (a weighted wheel that rotates back and forth, being returned toward its centre position by a spiral), were invented in Europe at around the start of the fourteenth century. They became the standard timekeeping device until the pendulum clock was invented in 1656. This remained the most accurate timekeeper until the 1930s, when quartz oscillators (where the mechanical **resonance** of a vibrating crystal is used to create an electrical signal with a very precise **frequency**) were invented, followed by atomic clocks after World War Two. Although initially limited to laboratories, the development of microelectronics in the 1960s made **quartz clocks** both compact and cheap to produce, and by the 1980s they became the world's dominant timekeeping technology in both clocks and **wristwatches**.

The concept of the wristwatch goes back to the production of the very earliest watches in the sixteenth century. Elizabeth I of England received a wristwatch from Robert Dudley in 1571, described as an arm watch. From the beginning, they were almost exclusively worn by women, while men used pocket-watches up until the early twentieth century. This was not just a matter of fashion or prejudice; watches of the time were notoriously prone to fouling from exposure to the elements, and could only reliably be kept safe from harm if carried securely in the pocket. Wristwatches were first worn by military men towards the end of the nineteenth century, when the importance of synchronizing manoeuvres during war without potentially revealing the plan to the enemy through signalling was increasingly recognized. It was clear that using pocket watches while in the heat of battle or while mounted on a horse was impractical, so officers began to strap the watches to their wrist.

The company H. Williamson Ltd., based in Coventry, England, was one of the first to capitalize on this opportunity. During the company's 1916 AGM it was noted that '...the public is buying the practical things of life. Nobody can truthfully contend that the watch is a luxury. It is said that one soldier in every four wears a wristlet watch, and the other three mean to get one as soon as they can.' By the end of the War, almost all enlisted men wore a wristwatch, and after they were demobilized, the fashion soon caught on - the British *Horological Journal* wrote in 1917 that '...the wristlet watch was little used by the sterner sex before the war, but now is seen on the wrist of nearly every man in uniform and of many men in civilian attire.' Within a decade, sales of wristwatches had outstripped those of pocket watches.

Now that clocks and watches had become 'common objects' there was a massively increased demand on clockmakers for maintenance and repair. Julien Le Roy, a clockmaker of Versailles, invented a face that could be opened to view the inside clockwork – a development which many subsequent artisans copied. He also invented special repeating mechanisms to improve the precision of clocks and supervised over 3,500 watches. The more complicated the device however, the more often it needed repairing. Today, since almost all clocks are now factory-made, most modern clockmakers *only* repair clocks. They are frequently employed by jewellers, antique shops or places devoted strictly to repairing clocks and watches.

The clockmakers of the present must be able to read blueprints and instructions for numerous types of clocks and time pieces that vary from antique clocks to modern time pieces in order to fix and make clocks or watches. The trade requires fine motor coordination as clockmakers must frequently work on devices with small gears and fine machinery, as well as an appreciation for the original art form. As is evident from this very short history of clocks and watches, over the centuries the items themselves have changed – almost out of recognition, but the importance of time-keeping has not. It is an area which provides a constant source of fascination and scientific discovery, still very much evolving today. We hope the reader enjoys this book.

PREFACE

THE Author wishes to express his thanks to the following firms who have kindly lent blocks for illustrations : Messrs. Gillett & Johnston, Croydon ; Messrs. Gent & Co., Leicester ; Messrs. James Ritchie & Son, Edinburgh ; and The Synchronome Co., London.

Figs. 1, 4, and 16 have been reproduced, with the kind permission of Messrs. E. & F. N. Spon, from F. J. Britten's *Watch and Clock Makers' Handbook, Dictionary, and Guide;* and among other works which have been consulted, and to which the reader is referred for more detailed information than can be included in the present book, are : *Rees's Cyclopaedia* ; E. J. Wood's *Curiosities of Clocks and Watches* ; Cescinsky and Webster's *English Domestic Clocks* ; F. J. Britten's *Old Clocks and Watches and their Makers* ; D. Glasgow's *Watch and Clock Making* ; Lord Grimthorpe's *Clocks, Watches, and Bells* ; Saunier's *Treatise on Modern Horology.*

CONTENTS

CHAP.		PAGE
	PREFACE	V
I.	TIME	1
II.	PRIMITIVE METHODS OF TIME MEASUREMENT	10
III.	THE PENDULUM AND CLOCK ESCAPEMENTS	25
IV.	THE BALANCE SPRING AND WATCH ESCAPEMENTS	40
V.	GENERAL MECHANISMS	52
VI.	STRIKING MECHANISMS	66
VII.	TEMPERATURE COMPENSATION	73
VIII.	THE CHRONOMETER AND FAMOUS ENGLISH HOROLOGISTS	83
IX.	CLOCK AND WATCH CASES	93
X.	ELECTRIC CLOCKS	99
XI.	TRADE	117
	INDEX	125

ILLUSTRATIONS

	LARGE TOWER CLOCK	*Frontispiece*
FIG.		PAGE
1.	ANCIENT CLEPSYDRA	14
2.	SEVENTEENTH-CENTURY WATER CLOCK	15
3.	EARLY VERGE ESCAPEMENT	18
4.	FUSEE	22
5.	RECOIL ESCAPEMENT	30
6.	DEAD-BEAT ESCAPEMENT	32
7.	OBSERVATORY CLOCK	38
8.	HORIZONTAL ESCAPEMENT	41
9.	LEVER ESCAPEMENT	44
10.	CLOCK TRAIN	53
11.	GENEVA STOP	58
12.	SWISS KEYLESS MECHANISM	62
13.	LOCKING PLATE	67
14.	SNAIL	68
15.	GRIDIRON PENDULUM	74
16.	COMPENSATION BALANCES	79
17.	CHRONOMETER ESCAPEMENT	89
18.	R. L. JONES'S SYNCHRONIZED PENDULUM	104
19.	RITCHIE'S REVERSED ESCAPEMENT	106
20.	"REFLEX" PENDULUM CONTROL	106
21.	FORCIBLE CORRECTION DEVICE	107
22.	SYNCHRONOME MASTER CLOCK	108
23.	SYNCHRONOME IMPULSE DIAL	109
24.	PULSYNETIC TRANSMITTER	111
25.	PULSYNETIC IMPULSE CLOCK	112
26.	THORNBRIDGE TRANSMITTER	113
27.	WAITING TRAIN MOVEMENT	114

CLOCKS AND WATCHES

CHAPTER I

TIME

FROM the common-sense standpoint, everyone understands, or considers that he understands, what is meant by time or duration; but an appreciation of its real nature, with its assumed infinite duration in the past and its infinity in the future, has always baffled the philosopher. According to Newton, absolute, true and mathematical time, by itself, flows uniformly on without respect to anything external. He thus conceived time as something which would continue even if there were no other physical phenomena, no material bodies, and no human being in existence. No method, however, can be imagined whereby such absolute time could be directly measured, and it is clear that for time measurement it is necessary to consider other physical changes in addition to time itself.

The change with which time can be most conveniently associated for this purpose is motion, and time-measurement is based upon the observation of a standard uniform motion, the rotation of the earth on its axis being that actually employed.

The theory of relativity, with which Einstein's name is associated, has recently attracted consiaerable attention, and it includes an idea of time quite different from that enunciated by Newton. According to this theory, there is no universal absolute time, and the measurements of both time and length will vary with the motion of the observer making the measurements. Two observers on different moving systems will fail to agree as to what constitute equal periods of time or equal lengths of bodies, and they will not always agree as to whether two events occur simultaneously or otherwise, even after corrections have been applied for the time taken by light to travel from the observed bodies to the observers. Measurements of the velocity of light, however, give the same result for both observers. The differences between the measurements of time and length by the two observers are quite inappreciable for motions relatively to one another which come within the range of human experience, and no practical difficulties, in connection with clocks and watches, arise from this theory.

The rotation of the earth, upon which practical time measurement is based, is determined by the apparent motions of the heavenly bodies, and some acquaintance with astronomical principles is necessary to appreciate the methods employed.

Although the stars are at different distances from the earth, they can all be imagined as projected upon a sphere of which the earth forms the centre, the size of the earth being so small in comparison with the distances of the stars that it can be taken as a point for this purpose. If the line joining the north and south poles of the earth be continued in both directions, the points where it would intersect this imaginary celestial sphere are the celestial poles ; and the circle half-way between the two poles, which divides the sphere into two equal portions, is the celestial equator. Just as a place on the earth's surface is determined by its latitude and longitude, so is the position of a star on the celestial sphere determined by its declination and right ascension. The declination is the angular distance north or south of the celestial equator, while the right ascension corresponds with terrestrial longitude. The longitude of a place on the earth's surface is the angle between the meridian of that place and the meridian of Greenwich, and is measured east or west up to 180°. In measuring the right ascension of a star, reference is made to the celestial meridian passing through the first point of Aries, which is the position of the sun at the commencement of spring (about 21st March); and the right ascension of a star is the angle between the meridian of the first point of Aries and the meridian of the star. It is measured, however, to the east only from 0° to 360°; usually it is expressed in time and not in degrees, twenty-four hours being equal to 360°.

The rotation of the earth on its axis once a day causes the stars to have an apparent motion round the celestial poles in an opposite direction, that is, east to west. When a star crosses the meridian of a place, it is said to transit; and the time occupied by the same star between two successive transits over the same meridian is a sidereal day.

The sidereal day at any place commences at sidereal noon, when the first point of Aries is on the meridian. The instant at which this occurs is taken as 0 hours, and the sidereal day is counted from 0 to 24 hours, sidereal or star time. This is a very convenient system for many astronomical observations; for example, the right ascension of a star on the meridian of a place is the sidereal time at that place, and every observatory possesses a sidereal clock; but it is not a suitable system for ordinary requirements. At different portions of the year, sidereal noon occurs at different times of the day and night, and for ordinary purposes a time system in which the noon has an approximately fixed relationship to the periods of daylight and darkness is desirable.

The positions of the stars with respect to one another on the celestial sphere remain very nearly constant, but this does not apply to the sun. Although the sun joins with the stars in partaking of the daily motion from east to west caused by the earth's rotation on its axis, an additional motion of the sun in an opposite direction can be observed, which is due to the earth revolving in its orbit round the sun. This causes the sun to move from the west to the east among the stars and to return to the same position after a period of a year. This annual movement of the sun among the stars cannot be directly noticed by an ordinary observer, as the stars are not visible at daytime ; but astronomers know the sun's declination and right ascension, and it can thus be inferred that it is adjacent to stars having about the same declination and right ascension, although the stars cannot at the time be actually seen. Owing to the fact that the axis upon which the earth rotates once a day is not perpendicular to the plane in which it revolves round the sun once a year, the path of the sun among the stars is not along the celestial equator, but along a path known as the ecliptic, the plane of which is inclined to the plane of the equator at an angle of about $23\frac{1}{2}°$.

The apparent solar day is the interval between two successive transits of the sun at any place, and in apparent solar time the noon is taken as the instant of the sun's transit. Like sidereal time, however, apparent solar time is not suitable for modern everyday use. By comparing the lengths of solar days at different times of the year, it is found that they vary in length. This is due to two reasons : (a) the path or orbit in which the earth revolves round the sun once a year is elliptical and, as the earth moves more quickly when it is near the sun, the apparent motion of the latter among the stars is not uniform ; (b) as already explained, the sun's motion among the stars is along the ecliptic, which is inclined to the celestial equator, and, although uniform motion of the sun along the equator would result in successive solar days being equal, this does not apply to motion in the inclined ecliptic ; and even if the motion of the sun in the ecliptic were uniform, the solar days would still be unequal.

To overcome the difficulty arising from these unequal solar days, the mean solar day has been introduced. The length of this day is the average of all the apparent solar days of a year ; and for determining mean solar time, an imaginary body known as the mean sun is assumed, which is supposed to move uniformly along the celestial equator. The time at which this imaginary body would transit the meridian of a place is the local mean noon of that place, and the interval between two successive mean noons is a mean solar day. This day is divided into twenty-four hours, which are subdivided into minutes and seconds ; and mean time is that used for ordinary purposes.

The mean noons of places in different meridians occur at different instants, and the local mean time of places more to the west is consequently behind those to the east. In order that there may be agreement in the time used over areas of countries, it is necessary to select some standard ; and Greenwich mean time, the noon of which is the instant at which the mean sun transits the meridian of Greenwich, is the standard time used in Great Britain, France, Belgium, and Spain. For other longitudes, the meridians successively an additional 15° east or west of Greenwich are taken ; and the standard time of a place is, in general, the mean solar time of the nearest standard meridian. Thus Norway, Sweden, Germany, Austria, and Italy employ the meridian 15° east, the time corresponding to which is exactly one hour in advance of Greenwich mean time ; while the United States of America employ four meridians—75°, 90°, 105°, and 120° west—giving times five, six, seven, and eight hours behind Greenwich time, and known as eastern, central, mountain, and Pacific times respectively.

The Civil mean day commences at midnight, and is counted from 0 to 12 hours at mid-day and then again from 0 to 12 midnight, although a system of reckoning from 0 midnight to 24 hours the next midnight is employed on Continental railways, and has been frequently suggested for general use in this and other countries It was used in the British Army, towards the end of the war, in 1918.

The Astronomical day is counted in 24 hours, commencing at noon, so that 8 p.m., 26th February, civil time is 8 hours, 26th February, astronomical time ; but 8 a.m., 27th February, civil time is 20 hours, 26th February, astronomical time. This system of beginning the day at noon is in accordance with the method used in sidereal time, and it seems to have been found to be convenient by astronomers and navigators. There is, however, some danger of confusion, and it has recently been decided that the Astronomical and Civil days shall agree. Commencing in 1925, the *Nautical Almanac* tables will be arranged with reference to days commencing at midnight, that is, the Astronomical day will after that date agree with the Civil day.

Dealing with civil time only, any particular date is used at different parts of the earth to cover a period of time extending over 48 hours. For example, at a place such as Fiji, nearly 180° east longitude, Saturday, 1st January, 1921, commenced at midnight when it was 12 noon Friday, 31st December, 1920, Greenwich mean time ; while for a place nearly 180° west longitude, 1st January ended when it was 12 noon Sunday, 2nd January, Greenwich mean time. As might be expected under such conditions, there is a possibility of mistakes being made when meteorological and other observations at different parts of the world are being correlated, and it has been suggested that Greenwich mean time should be employed as a universal time for such observations.

A year is the time taken by the earth to move in its orbit once round the sun and, as has been already stated, this movement results in an apparent motion of the sun along the ecliptic among the stars. The plane of the ecliptic is inclined to that of the celestial equator at an angle of about 23° 27′ and cuts the equator at two points, 180° apart. One point is the first point of Aries, and is the position occupied by the sun at the commencement of spring or the vernal equinox ; while the other is the autumnal equinox.

A tropical year is the interval between two successive vernal equinoces, and is equal to 365 days 5 hrs. 48 mins. 49·7 secs. mean solar time, that is, a little less than $365\frac{1}{4}$ days. As the sun has moved from west to east, with respect to the stars, once round the celestial sphere during this period, it follows that the stars have made about $366\frac{1}{4}$ revolutions relatively to the earth, and that $365\frac{1}{4}$ mean solar days are equal to about $366\frac{1}{4}$ sidereal days. Twenty-four sidereal hours are thus equal to 23 hrs. 56 mins. 4·1 secs. mean time, and the sidereal noon is about 4 mins. mean time earlier each day than on the preceding day.

Modern methods of timekeeping are still based on astronomical observations to check the accuracy of clocks ; but it may be mentioned that the time of rotation of the earth is not perfectly uniform, each day being very slightly longer than the day preceding it, and more permanent standards of time have been suggested for which, before the introduction of the modern relativity theory, constancy throughout all space and time were claimed. It is estimated that, considered as a clock, the earth loses about 22 secs. in 100 years.

Although our definition of mean time is obtained from the apparent motion of the sun, star observations are those usually employed for checking time, the sidereal day being, in fact, the actual standard from which the mean solar day and its divisions into hours, minutes, and seconds are determined.

At one time it was usual for a person to check the accuracy of his watch by comparison with a sun dial. John Smith, in his *Horological Dialogues* published in 1675, warned his readers to set their watches continuously by the same dial, otherwise owing to the different readings of the dials they might be misled as to the performance of their watches. To-day it is not necessary for each person to resort to a direct astronomical comparison to correct his watch, as telegraphic transmission has rendered it possible for the astronomers at Greenwich to transmit time signals all over the country.

A time signal is transmitted automatically every hour from the mean solar clock at Greenwich Observatory to the Post Office, and from there time signals are distributed to various places. Arrangements can be made for these signals, which consist of electric currents, so to act that they will forcibly correct the clocks of subscribers, or they may merely release a falling ball or deflect a galvanometer needle, and give an indication of value in determining the error and rate of a chronometer or watch.

CHAPTER II

PRIMITIVE METHODS OF TIME MEASUREMENT

ONE of the earliest methods of determining the time was by means of the shadow cast by the sun. There is a reference to an appliance embodying this principle in the thirty-eighth chapter of Isaiah (v. 8), and there are other historical accounts of greater antiquity.

If a vertical rod were placed at the north or the south pole of the earth, with its lower end fixed on a horizonal circle or dial, the shadow of the rod cast by the sun would move round the dial, and the edge of the circle could be simply divided into twenty-four equal portions to indicate solar hours. The variations in the declination of the sun, due to its moving in the ecliptic, would cause its altitude, or angular distance above the horizon, to alter; and although this would produce variations in the length of the shadow, it would not affect the direction and, during the portion of the year when the sun is visible at the pole concerned, the arrangement would serve its purpose.

Such, however, is not the case at other latitudes. If the vertical rod were mounted in London, it could be used to indicate solar noon, as its shadow would always be in a northerly direction when the sun's bearing was south. But at other times of the day the sun's bearing depends not only on the solar time, but also on the sun's declination. Thus at 3 p.m. in midsummer the sun's bearing would be about 22° south of west, while at 3 p.m. mid-winter it would be about 50° south of west, and the direction of the shadow of the rod at any time of the day would consequently vary with the seasons. This change is due to the fact that in mid-summer the sun is $23\frac{1}{2}°$ north of the celestial equator, while in mid-winter it is $23\frac{1}{2}°$ south of that equator. If, however, in London we erect our rod or "gnomon" so that it is parallel to the rod we imagined to be erected at one of the earth's poles, that is, it is parallel to the earth's axis, the variations in the sun's declination will no longer affect the direction of the shadow, and we can use the same graduated dial to indicate solar time throughout all days of the year, provided, of course, the sun is not obscured by clouds or fogs. The graduated divisions corresponding to intervals of a solar hour will not, however, be equal to one another.

As the altitude of the celestial pole is equal to the latitude of the observer, the rod must be inclined to the horizontal at an angle equal to the latitude, which for London is 50° 30′.

Instead of a rod, sun dials usually employ a wedge-shaped piece, or gnomon, fixed in a vertical plane on the horizontal graduated dial, the edge of wedge corresponding with the rod. The plane of the dial can, however, be varied if the graduations are suitably altered, and sun dials on vertical walls are frequently employed.

Portable sun dials were used before the general introduction of watches, and they included a magnetic compass to enable the gnomon to be placed in a north and south direction.

The time indicated by a sun dial is local solar time, and to obtain the local mean time it is necessary to apply a correction known as the "equation of time." The two reasons for the differences of these times are stated on pages 4-5, and the corrections to be applied on any day are given in the *Nautical* and *Whitaker's*

Almanacks. On some days, when the sun is "after the clock," the equation of time is added to sun dial time to get mean time; but when the sun is "before the clock," the amount is subtracted. If Greenwich mean time is required, it is necessary to make a further correction for the longitude of the place of observation.

The equation of time is zero four days a year (about 15th April, 14th June, 1st Sept., and 25th Dec.), and on these days the interval between the sun's rising and mean noon is practically equal to the interval between mean noon and the sun's setting; but when the sun is before the clock, the former interval is greater than the latter. Thus about the beginning of November, when the equation of time reaches its maximum value of about 16 mins. 20 secs., the sun rises at London at about 6.57 a.m. and sets about 4.30 p.m. mean time. The period from sunrise to mean noon is then 5 hrs. 3 mins. and from noon to sunset 4 hrs. 30 mins., the difference 33 mins. being about twice the equation of time. The opposite effect is produced when the sun is after the clock, and the after-mean-noon period of daylight is then longer than the forenoon period.

In recent years, civil time has been advanced one hour during the summer months, which has the effect of putting the sun one hour more behind the summer-time clock than the equation of time would place it behind a mean time clock, so that about 26th July—when the equation of time is 6 mins. 17 secs., to be added to apparent solar time—the total correction to be applied to the sun dial to obtain the new summer time is 1 hr. 6 mins. 17 secs., and the after-summer-time-noon period of daylight is about 2 hrs. 12 mins. longer than the morning period.

Water clocks, or clepsydrae, are very ancient devices

for measuring time, and it is even uncertain whether or not their use preceded that of sun dials. Their action depends upon the flow of water through an orifice; and in one primitive form the water passed from one vessel into another which was provided with a float, the position of which indicated the time. One ancient form consisted of a small copper bowl, which floated in a vessel of water until the water, leaking through a small hole in the bottom of the bowl, caused it to sink after a certain interval of time.

For any approach to uniformity in the rate of flow of the water, it is essential that the pressure head, or vertical distance between the surface of the fluid and the orifice, should be constant, and in ancient forms this condition was obtained by keeping the reservoir full and allowing water to run to waste.

Another difficulty which had to be overcome arose from the primitive method of counting the hours. The day was taken as extending from sunrise to sunset, and both this period and the time of darkness were divided into twelve equal parts. The hours consequently varied in length in different seasons of the year, and during daylight and darkness; but the inconvenience arising from such an arrangement would not be so considerable in places nearer to the equator as in more northerly latitudes. The idea of taking a fixed time, such as the middle of the night, for the purpose of counting the hours, was a complication involving calculations, and did not suggest itself so obviously to the ancients as the definite phenomenon of sunrise. Even in ancient times, however, the division into equal hours was used by astronomers, being probably introduced by the Babylonians. The period from midnight to midnight was divided into twenty-four equal hours, but these equal hours do not appear to have come into general use until clocks were introduced in the fourteenth century.

Fig. 1 represents an ancient clepsydra of about 200 B.C., which is said to be due to Ctesibius of Alexandria (Ctesibius was a famous inventor, and was the son of a barber). Water passes from a reservoir through a pipe H into a cone A, from which it passes drop by drop through a regulated orifice into the cylinder E. The water in the cone is kept at a constant level, I being an overflow pipe. B is a conical plug fitting into A, and serves the purpose of regulating the rate of flow of the water from A into E. When B is raised, the water passes more quickly; and B is attached to the rod D, by means of which it can be raised or lowered to its correct position corresponding with the time of the year and with whether it is daytime or night. Within the chamber E there is a float carrying a vertical rack, which gears with a toothed wheel. Upon this wheel a pointer is mounted, which indicates the time.

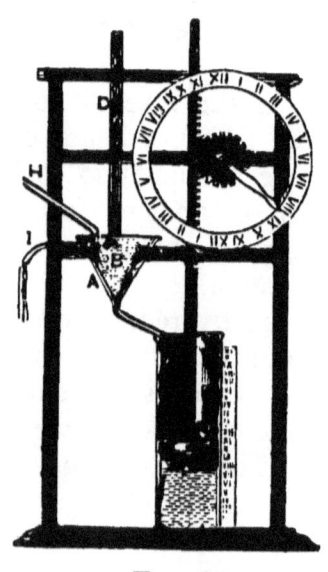

FIG. 1

This appliance required adjustments of the position of the regulating plug every sunrise and sunset, but in a later modification an automatic arrangement was obtained.

In this case, water was maintained at a constant level in a reservoir, from which it passed drop by drop, at a uniform rate, through a pipe into a chamber containing a float. The latter carried a figure of a man holding a spear, the point of which indicated the hour on a graduated scale. Connected with the chamber, there was a siphon and, when at the end of twenty-four hours the chamber was filled, this siphon came into action, and the whole of the water was discharged from the chamber. The float then fell to its lowest position, and the spear again pointed to the bottom of the scale.

The discharged water passed from the siphon on to a water wheel below, and its weight caused the wheel to turn through one-sixth of a revolution. The wheel, which thus rotated once in six days, carried a pinion gearing with a contrate wheel, on the axis of which there was another pinion engaging with a toothed wheel, which carried a cylinder upon which the graduated scale indicating the hours was marked.

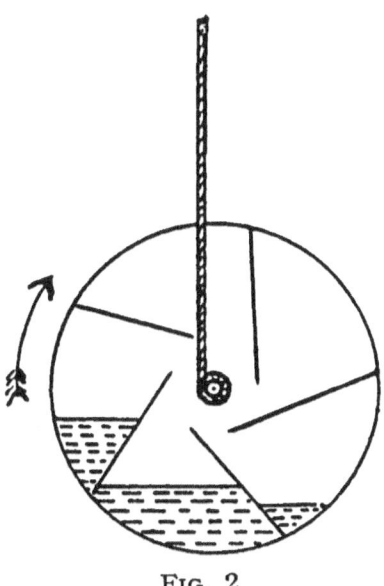

FIG. 2

The numbers of the teeth of the wheels and pinions were such that this cylinder rotated once in a year. The graduated scale drawn on the cylindrical surface took the form of a series of twenty-four lines with varying inclinations, which passed round the cylinder, and it was so arranged that on any particular day the varying intervals between the successive lines facing the spear corresponded to the varying lengths of the successive hours.

Fig. 2 illustrates a form of water clock which was

introduced about the middle of the seventeenth century, when it was no longer necessary to arrange for different lengths of hours. A hermetically-sealed metal drum, about 5 ins. diameter, contained a small quantity of water, and was divided by a number of partitions as shown in the sectional drawing. An axle projects from the centres of the flat ends of the drum, and the whole was suspended by means of two cords attached to the axle. When the drum was wound up, the cords were wrapped round the axles, and the water fell over the inner and open edges of the partitions into the lowest portions of the drum. The weight of the drum tended to make it descend; while the weight of the water in the bottom part opposed this motion, because the rotation of the drum in its descent would, in the first place, involve lifting this water to a higher level. As, however, the partitions contained a certain number of perforations through which the water could pass from one chamber to another, the drum could descend slowly and the position of the axle was used to indicate the time on a vertical scale, which was mounted upon the stand to which the supporting cords were attached.

If fine sand be used instead of water, the rate of flow is independent of the height of the column employed, and appliances embodying this principle have been extensively used in the past. They are a later invention than either sun dials or clepsydrae, and were probably introduced about 1,600 years ago.

A sand-glass or an hour-glass consists of a double-chambered vessel, the two chambers being connected at the waist by an orifice. The waist is contracted into the form of a double cone, the inclination of which agrees with the angle of repose of the sand, that is, the angle at the side of a pile of sand which just remains at rest without any tendency of the sand to slip down

PRIMITIVE METHODS OF TIME MEASUREMENT

the pile. The sand passes under the action of gravity from the upper to the lower chamber, and the whole is inverted when the glass is again used. Usually they are designed to indicate the passage of the time required for the upper chamber to empty itself, and appliances of this nature have been used in connection with navigation, and also in pulpits and kitchens, more especially in the latter case to indicate the time required to boil an egg.

King Alfred is said to have introduced the use of burning candles to measure time. Asser, his biographer, states that he used a candle 12 ins. long, divided by marks into twelve divisions. Each candle lasted four hours, six being used in the twenty-four hours of a complete day, and it was specified that the weight of the wax from which the six candles were made was to be equal to that of seventy-two pennies. As it was found that the wind blew the candle out, the latter was surrounded by a lantern built up of wood and horn plates.

At a later date, oil clocks were used in which the amount of unburnt oil left in a graduated reservoir of a lamp indicated the time.

These primitive methods do not approach the accuracy now obtainable by mechanical means, although a simple modification of a sun dial, known as a meridian dial, can sometimes be profitably employed, when the sun is on the meridian, for determining local solar noon.

There are doubtful references to weight-driven clocks as early as the ninth and tenth centuries, and it may be that some of these examples consisted of trains of wheels driven by weights and ending in a rotating fly with faces subjected to the resistance due to the air. Confusion arises from the practice of the early writers, who used the word "horologium" to indicate any appliance connected with timekeeping; and it is, consequently, sometimes difficult to distinguish between sun dials, clepsydrae, and mechanical contrivances. It seems probable, however, that it was not until the fourteenth century that clocks with escapements were introduced, the first form of escapement being the "verge."

The weight then drove a series of wheels ending in a crown wheel with a horizontal axis and pointed teeth (*see* Fig. 3), which engaged with projecting faces or "pallets" on a vertical arbor or verge carrying an arm, on the ends of which weights were mounted. This was known as a foliot balance. One of the pointed teeth pressed against one of the pallets and thus caused the balance to rotate until the tooth escaped past the edge of the pallet, and the crown wheel was then free to turn until a tooth approximately opposite to the tooth last in action engaged with the other pallet. The pressure of this tooth opposed the existing motion of the balance and gradually brought it to rest, the wheel train being driven backward or made to "recoil" during this process. Subsequently the balance was forced to rotate in the opposite direction. In this fashion, the train of wheels moved through the space of half a wheel tooth of the crown wheel for each swing of the balance.

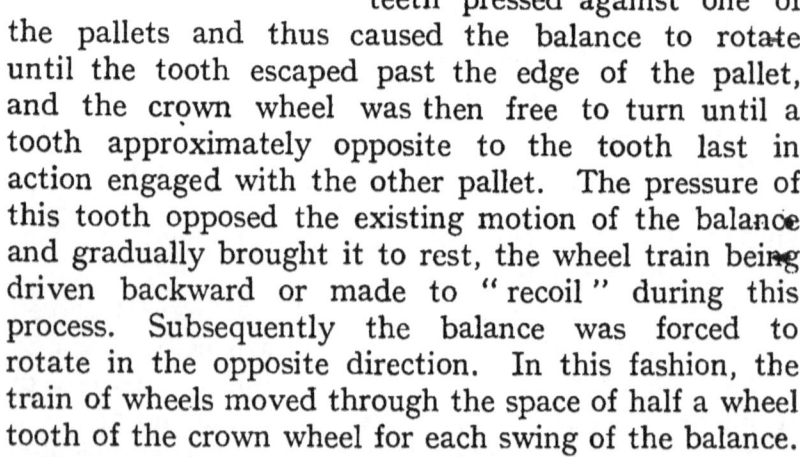

FIG. 3

The time of vibration varied considerably and depended on the force exerted by the wheel teeth, on the weights carried by the balance, and on their distance from the axis. By adjusting the latter distance, the clock could be regulated, as it would go slower if the weights were placed at a greater distance from the centre. Accurate timekeeping depended upon constancy in the driving force, a condition which could not be relied upon, for one reason, owing to the change with time in the lubricant. Mechanically, there are several objections to the arrangement. When a tooth of the crown wheel engages with a pallet, the two are moving in opposite direction and, consequently, meet in a violent manner, which results in grooves or pits being formed in the pallets, besides destroying the points of the wheel teeth.

In spite of the objections, this device should be regarded with considerable respect, as it marks one of the most important steps in the development of our subject. Many clocks were made on this principle before the middle of the seventeenth century.

Early clocks were often provided with mechanical contrivances which are absent from all but a few modern clocks. Some of these contrivances were very complicated and indicated astronomical phenomena, while, in others, automatic figures were employed to strike the hours and sometimes to give short dramatic performances. One of the earliest clocks made in England is that said to have been constructed by Peter Lightfoot, about 1335, when he was a resident monk at Glastonbury Abbey. It was installed in the abbey church, but at the time of the dissolution of the monastery—in the reign of Henry VIII—it appears to have been removed to Wells Cathedral, where part of it still remains. The dial is about 6 ft. 6 ins. in diameter and is mounted in a square frame, at each corner of which is a representation of an angel holding the head of a man. The outer circle of the dial is painted blue, with gilt stars on it. It is divided into twenty-four equal parts, representing the hours in two series of twelve, mid-day and midnight being indicated by a cross instead of a number. In place of a pointer, there is a gilt star or sun, which traverses the dial and indicates the hours. An inner circle is graduated to show the minutes by means of a smaller traversing star, and within this circle there is a third marked to show the age of the moon in days. The phases of the moon are also represented through a hole in a middle plate.

Above the dial there is an arched piece, from the base of which an octagonal platform projects, and over the middle of the platform there is a panelled turret, on each side of which there are two knights mounted on horses. By means of a separate weight and a detent-releasing gear, it is arranged that when the clock strikes the hours, the two knights on one side charge their opponents on the other as in a tournament. Other moving figures were provided, including a man within the church, who is connected by rods with the clock, and strikes the quarters with his feet on two small bells; while for the hours he is provided with a battle-axe, with which he strikes another bell.

It is more than doubtful whether the figures now to be seen are the originals, and in 1835 the clock itself was considered to be worn out. A new one was supplied by Messrs. Thwaites & Reed, of Clerkenwell, London. The dial and the moving figures were, however, adapted to the new movement.

The old movement is now exhibited in the Western Galleries of the Science Museum South Kensington, and is still in motion. Originally it had a verge escapement; but following upon the introduction of the pendulum in the seventeenth century, an anchor escapement and pendulum were substituted. The frame and the original wheels are of iron, and the framework is secured by means of cotters.

The striking work is driven by separate weights, and is of the locking-plate type still used for turret clocks.

Another clock in the Science Museum shows the original verge escapement employed in the fourteenth century. This example is of Swiss manufacture, and is said to have been made in the year 1348. It was formerly in Dover Castle. The crown wheel of the escapement has thirty-three teeth, and the pallets on the verge make an angle of about 100 degrees with one another. The cross-bar or foliot balance is partly suspended by a cord to lessen the friction in the bottom pivot.

About 1364 or 1370, a German, Henry de Vick (or Wyck), made a clock of a similar type for Charles V of France, which was placed in the tower of the latter's palace ; and drawings of this clock, with descriptions, will be found in *Rees's Cyclopaedia*.

At the present time, the word " clock " is applied generally to all time-keepers other than pocket watches and ships' chronometers ; but the word is derived from the German and French equivalents for bell, and, strictly speaking, " clock " should be used only with reference to striking and alarm clocks. No special importance need be attached to this distinction, but it should be noted that clockmakers still observe the difference and refer to non-striking clocks as timepieces.

The introduction of a mainspring for driving the wheel train is ascribed to Peter Hele, of Nuremberg, about or before 1500, and this invention rendered practicable the construction of portable clocks and watches, which included a verge escapement of the form already described.

The mainspring consisted of a coiled strip of steel, and the force obtained from it varied considerably with the amount it was wound up. With the escapement employed, accuracy of timekeeping depended on a constant driving force, and the watch would go faster when fully wound up than when run down. To lessen the variations of the driving force, an early device known as a "stackfreed" was employed. This consisted of a cam which engaged with a stiff strip spring, the whole being so arranged that at its greatest tension the mainspring gave up energy to the strip spring ; and that, later, when the mainspring exerted its smallest force, its action was assisted by the strip spring.

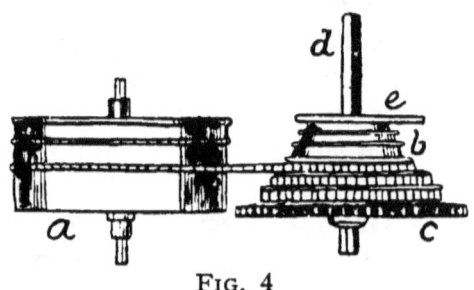

Fig. 4

A better device is that supposed to have been introduced by Jacob Zech, of Prague, in 1525, and known as the fusee. In this arrangement (*see* Fig. 4), the barrel, *a*, containing the spring was connected by a gut (later by a chain) with the fusee, which consisted of a tapering piece, *b*, with a spiral groove cut on it, and its varying diameters gave the necessary changes of leverage to compensate for the varying pull of the spring. The spring is coiled up within the barrel, and the latter turns upon a fixed middle piece known as the barrel arbor, which is provided with a hook fitting into a hole near the inner end of the spring. The outer end of the spring generally has a similar hole, which

PRIMITIVE METHODS OF TIME MEASUREMENT

embraces a hook on the inside of the barrel itself. The spring is wound up by rotating the fusee, the connecting cord transmitting the motion to the barrel. When the spring is "run down," its coils are in close contact with one another near the rim of the barrel; but when it is fully wound up, they are crowded together near the barrel arbor at the centre.

When a spring in the form of a flat spiral is wound up, the moment of the force with which it tends to unwind itself is proportional to the angle through which it has been wound up, provided the outer extremity of the spring has not bent inwards; and the shape of the longitudinal section of the fusee would theoretically take the form of a curve known as a rectangular hyperbola. The condition mentioned is not usually complied with, and the matter is also complicated by the friction which may exist between adjacent coils of the spring. In actual practice, it is necessary to adjust the shape of the fusee by trial.

Until recent times, fusees were fitted to almost all English watches, and are still used in chronometers.

In the earliest watches, the frames and the wheels were made of iron or steel, and generally they were designed to strike the hours. Before the invention of the balance spring in the seventeenth century, the standard of timekeeping must have been very low; and Edward J. Wood, in his interesting book *Curiosities of Clocks and Watches*, repeats a story in this connection. The Emperor Charles V of Austria, about the middle of the sixteenth century, after his abdication, used to sit after dinner with several watches or small table-clocks on the table before him, his bottle being in the centre. He endeavoured " to amuse his dejected mind by trying to make his portable clocks accord—a vain task, as he found, and productive only of a salutary moral reflection in his brain, which shaped itself in the following pithy words : ' What an egregious fool must I have been to have squandered so much blood and treasure in an absurd attempt to make all men think alike, when I cannot even make a few watches keep time together.' "

CHAPTER III

THE PENDULUM AND CLOCK ESCAPEMENTS

ALTHOUGH there are accounts of the pendulum having been used in earlier times, the credit of the discovery of its fundamental property is usually given to Galileo, who, in 1582, is said to have noticed that the lamps suspended by chains in the cathedral at Pisa occupied equal periods of time for swinging through arcs of unequal lengths. He checked his observations by counting the beats of his pulse, and one of the first uses of the pendulum is said to have been made by physicians, who carried a simple portable form, consisting of a ball and string, and adjusted the length of the string until the oscillations of the ball synchronized with the beats of a patient's pulse. By reference to a table of lengths, the rate of the pulse was ascertained.

For equal periods of vibration, independently of the lengths of the arcs, it is necessary that the force acting on the pendulum in the direction of its motion should, at any instant, be proportional to its distance from its middle position. The Dutch scientist, Christiaan Huygens, showed that instead of a circular path, a cycloidal path (that is, the curve described by a point on the circumference of a circle rolling on a straight line) was required; and the difference introduced in clocks by the departure from the cycloidal path is known as the "circular error." It is practically negligible if the arc is kept small enough, say two or three degrees on each side of the vertical; and the time of a single vibration is then obtained from the formula $t = \pi \sqrt{\frac{l}{g}}$ where t is the time of vibration in seconds, l is the length of the pendulum in feet, and g is the acceleration of gravity which, in London, is 32·2 ft. per second per second; thus for $t = 1$ sec., $l = 39\cdot14$ ins.

For a total angle of swing of 2°, that is, 1° on each side of the vertical, the circular error in twenty-four hours is equivalent to a loss of 1·6 secs.; while for a swing of 2° on each side of the vertical, which is about the usual angle in a good clock, the error amounts to 6·6 secs. in twenty-four hours; a swing of 5° on each side of the vertical involves a total loss of 41 secs. in the same time.

Even with a considerable circular error, accurate timekeeping is still possible if the arc is kept constant; as in a clock, we are not concerned with the total circular error, but only with the differences introduced by the variations of the arc. For example, a variation of $\frac{1}{4}°$ in the common half-arc of 2° would mean a loss or gain of about 3 secs. a day, and such a variation is much more than would occur in a good timepiece.

The preceding calculations apply to an imaginary simple pendulum, which would consist of a weightless thread supporting a weight concentrated at a point; and though a ball of lead suspended by a thread closely approaches the conditions (especially if the thread is long), it does not exactly fulfil them. The pendulums actually used in clocks are known as compound pendulums, and the bob is supported by a rod possessing weight. The whole consists of a number of particles at different distances from the centre of motion, and each particle tends to follow the simple pendulum law, with the result that the whole vibrates as though its mass were concentrated at a point which is below the centre of gravity of the whole pendulum. This point is known as the centre of oscillation, and it has the property that, if the pendulum were inverted and suspended from this point, the time of vibration would not be altered. The centre of gravity of the whole pendulum must not be confused with the centre of the bob, as the former is situated above the latter, owing to the weight of the rod. It sometimes happens, however—depending upon the shape and relative weights of the pendulum rod and bob—that the centre of oscillation coincides with the centre of gravity of the bob. The length of the pendulum is the distance between the point of suspension and the centre of oscillation.

There has been considerable controversy as to whom the credit is due for the first application of a pendulum to a clock. Following Galileo's discovery of the property of the pendulum, it was possible to measure small intervals of time by counting the swings; and, to avoid the necessity of continually counting, Galileo appears first to have devised a means of making the pendulum propel a train of wheels, which automatically recorded the number of swings; but the wheel work did not maintain the pendulum in motion, and it was necessary to apply external impulses to it whenever it nearly came to rest. At a later date, about 1641, when he was blind, he considered the possibility of applying pendulums to clocks driven by weights or springs, and discussed his ideas with his son Vincenzo. Between them they decided upon an arrangement, which was set out on a drawing; but Galileo died before his son commenced to make the clock.

A working model, showing the arrangement, is included in the Science Museum's collections.

There is also an account, of doubtful accuracy, that about 1641, Richard Harris erected a pendulum clock at St. Paul's Church, Covent Garden. Huygens, in

1657, devised a means of applying the pendulum. He suspended the latter by short cords placed between curved plates (cycloidal cheeks), which caused the bob of the pendulum to describe a cycloidal instead of a circular path, but this complication did not, in practice, prove to be desirable.

In the Gemeente Museum, at The Hague, there are portions of a turret clock from Scheveningen to which Huygens adapted the pendulum in 1658. The escape wheel was arranged as shown in the figure on page 18; but, instead of the foliot balance, there was an arm carrying a vertical pin, which engaged with a fork projecting from the pendulum.

A modern clock is designed to count the number of swings made by a pendulum, and is so arranged that there is as little interference as possible with the time of swing of the pendulum, owing to the impulses given by the clock mechanism to the pendulum to maintain it in vibration, and also owing to the checks on the pendulum's motion when it is actuating the clock mechanism to give the necessary record of the number of vibrations.

The train of clock wheels is urged forward by a weight or a spring; and, by means of a device known as an escapement, it is arranged that the train can only move forward through a certain interval for each swing of the pendulum. Pointers or hands are mounted on certain portions of the wheel train, which is so designed that these pointers indicate the time.

In applications of the pendulum to the verge escapement, the crown wheel was generally arranged with a vertical axis instead of a horizontal axis, and a short pendulum with a bob at its end was used instead of the older foliot balance. As the crown escape wheel was now at right angles to the wheel by which it was driven, it was necessary for the latter to be a contrate wheel, that is, a wheel with its teeth standing up perpendicularly to the plane of the wheel, instead of being arranged in the same plane. This device is seen in many bracket clocks of the seventeenth and eighteenth centuries. In some Dutch clocks, the crown wheel continued to be mounted on a horizontal axis, and the foliot balance was replaced by a horizontal wire bent at the end to engage with a long loop projecting from the pendulum.

In later applications, the pendulum, instead of being pivoted at the top, was suspended by means of a strip of spring, and had a slot which embraced a bent piece, named a fork, on the end of a rod which was connected with the verge and was known as a crutch. This method of supporting the pendulum and connecting it with the escapement is now generally employed, though sometimes modified.

With the verge escapement, it is obvious that the motion of the pendulum is always either in opposition to the action of the driving force of the train or under the action of that force, and that the ideal conditions of a free pendulum are far from being realized. In comparison with the earlier arrangement of a foliot balance, however, increased accuracy was attainable as equality in the times of the vibrations was no longer wholly dependent upon a constant driving force, the uniformity of the pendulum correcting to a considerable extent the defects of the escapement.

The invention of the anchor or recoil escapement by Robert Hooke or by William Clements, about 1675, marks an important step in the development of timekeeping. The escape wheel ceases to be of the crown-wheel type, and takes a flat form with a number of pointed teeth, which engage alternately with the pallet faces of the anchor, the latter being connected with the pendulum by a crutch and fork.

The action of the pointed teeth of the escape wheel on the inclined faces of the pallets will be understood from the sketch (Fig. 5).

A represents a block with an inclined face BC, and D is a rod pushed down with its end against BC. If A is fixed, the end of D will slide along the face BC; but if A is free and rests on a smooth surface, while D is constrained from moving sideways and must always keep in the same vertical line, then the effect of pushing down D would be to make A move to the right. In an escapement, D is represented by an escape wheel tooth, except that the latter is constrained to a circular instead of a straight path; while BC represents the inclined pallet face.

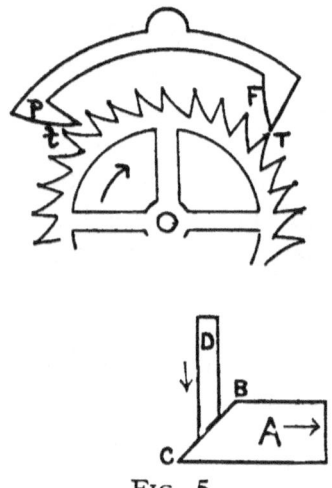

Fig. 5

In Fig. 5, which also shows the anchor escapement, when the tooth T engages with the inclined face F, it tends to make the pallet move to the right away from the central position until the tooth escapes past the edge of the face, as shown in the figure. The wheel is then free to move through a very small angle until another tooth t engages with the other pallet P. The anchor continues to move under the action of the pendulum and, owing to the shape of the pallets, the wheel is caused to recoil until the pendulum is brought to rest. The tooth t now pushes P away from the centre, and the process described is repeated.

THE PENDULUM AND CLOCK ESCAPEMENTS 31

Usually the acting faces of the pallets are convex in shape. During the greater part of each swing the wheel train is urging the pendulum forward, while at the end it opposes the pendulum's motion, so that some of the disadvantages of the verge escapement are still present. In fact, the anchor may be regarded as a modification of the verge, but the design is much more convenient and allows a spur wheel to be used instead of the contrate wheel ; while, as a smaller arc is practicable, a longer pendulum can be employed. It is sometimes insisted upon that the recoil prevents variations of the arc of vibration with variations of the driving force ; and, although this is true, it does not follow that constancy of arc essentially means constant time of vibration, as constancy of arc, if obtained with great departure from the ideal conditions of a free pendulum, may mean worse timekeeping than greater variations in which there is less interference with the free swing of the pendulum.

With this escapement, an increase in the driving force generally increases the arc of vibration ; but as the pendulum is made to move quicker, the time of this longer arc is less, although considerations of the circular error only would have led us to expect it to be longer. The circular error and the errors due to variations of the driving force thus act in opposite directions.

The dead-beat escapement invented by George Graham about 1715 affords a means of better timekeeping than any of its predecessors. It is an improved form of anchor escapement, and received the name " dead beat " owing to the escape wheel not being subjected to any recoil. The wheel advances through the space of half a tooth every time an impulse is given, and remains at rest during the intervals. Fig. 6 illustrates the device, one escape wheel tooth and the pallet with which it engages being shown on a larger scale. Instead of each pallet having only one acting face, as in the recoil escapement, there are two faces. One of these is inclined, and an escape wheel tooth engages with it to give an impulse; but when the pendulum and the pallets move so that the tooth escapes, the tooth next to come into action falls upon a locking face AB, which is circular in shape, with E as centre. The wheel then remains at rest, locked by AB, during the completion of the swing of the pendulum and also during the first part of the succeeding swing, until the pallets move and allow a tooth to engage with the impulse face BC. The pallet is then impelled to the right by the pressure of the wheel tooth until the latter escapes from BC, and another tooth then engages with the left-hand locking face, as shown in the figure. With the exception of a little friction between the wheel teeth and the circular or locking faces of the pallets, there is no interference with the free swing of the pendulum while the wheel is at rest, and that friction is reduced to a minimum by giving a high degree of finish to the acting surfaces. The disturbances of the pendulum due to the impulses are similarly reduced to a minimum by arranging that, as far as possible, the portions of the arc during which the impulses are given shall be bisected by the mid position of the pendulum. As, however, it is necessary in practice that the teeth shall fall on the locking surfaces, and not exactly at the corners of the locking

FIG. 6

THE PENDULUM AND CLOCK ESCAPEMENTS 33

surfaces and the impulse faces, that is, at B, the last condition cannot be fully realized.

An increase in the driving force increases the arc of swing, but, unlike the case with the recoil escapement, this causes the clock to lose, the loss being increased by the circular error. For this reason, the dead-beat escapement is not considered suitable for clocks that are liable to fluctuations in the driving force, and a half-dead-beat escapement is sometimes used in such cases. In that escapement the locking surfaces are designed to give a slight recoil, thus obtaining an action intermediate between the recoil and the dead-beat escapements. The latter is, however, used for astronomical and other high-class clocks or regulators for indoor use, while for ordinary English-made spring-driven clocks with short pendulums the recoil escapement has been preferred. A good regulator with a dead-beat escapement can be made to indicate the time to an accuracy of about one part in a million.

In large public clocks, where the hands are exposed to the winds, there may be considerable variations in the force acting upon the escapement, and the dead-beat escapement would not be the best to use under such circumstances. A half-dead-beat escapement, in which the teeth take the form of projecting pins, has sometimes been used.

One method of overcoming this difficulty is by employing a train remontoire, in which the main train is used to wind up at regular intervals a subsidiary driving system, which then drives the escapement independently of the main train, which alone is connected with the hands.

A better method is a gravity escapement, in which the impulses given to the pendulum remain constant, even though the load on the driving train varies. The impulses are not given directly to the pendulum by the train, but are given by means of arms which are raised through constant amounts by the action of the train, and these arms give impulses to the pendulum when they fall under the action of gravity.

Alexander Cummings and Thomas Mudge invented escapements of this type in the eighteenth century, and Lord Grimthorpe's double three-legged gravity escapement may be taken as a good example of the class. It is used for turret clocks, and was employed in the famous " Big Ben's " clock at Westminster, which was made in 1854. The escapement consists of two wheels, each with three long teeth or legs, mounted together on one axis, and having three lifting pins in the space between the two wheels. The pins engage with pallets mounted on hinged arms, which carry locking faces, while the bottom ends of the arms engage with the pendulum. One locking face projects forward from its arm and engages with the front wheel, while the other projects backward and engages with the back wheel. When the pendulum swings from its middle position to the right, it carries the right-hand locking face with it and releases the wheels, which rotate until the back wheel is stopped by the left-hand locking face. During this process, one of the lifting pins has engaged with the left-hand pallet and raised its arm through a small angle. When the pendulum next swings to the left, it engages with the left-hand arm and again causes a release of the wheels, which now move until the front wheel is locked, the right-hand gravity arm being slightly raised by one of the pins during this process. As the pendulum again swings to the right, the left-hand arm falls with it, and the angle through which it is in contact with the pendulum during this action is greater than the amount it has just been raised by the pendulum, the excess being the small angle through which the arm had been previously raised by the lifting pin. The energy corresponding to this small angle is the impulse given to the pendulum each swing, a similar series of actions taking place on both gravity arms.

A fly is mounted on the wheel axis to damp the motion of the wheels, and so prevent violent collisions between the teeth and the locking faces.

A large tower clock, with Grimthorpe's double three-legged gravity escapement, which was made by Messrs. Gillett & Johnston in 1913 for the Royal Courts of Justice, Pekin, is illustrated in the frontispiece, in which the escape wheel, the fly, and the gravity arms appear near the top of the middle portion. The clock strikes the hours, chimes the Westminster quarters, and drives the hands of four dials, 10 ft. in diameter. It has a nickel-steel pendulum beating $1\frac{1}{4}$ secs. and weighing 2 cwt.

The pendulums of clocks are suspended by strips of spring instead of being mounted on pivots, as in some of the early applications of the pendulum. This has the advantage of eliminating the friction at the pivots, and it also causes the path of the bob of the pendulum to follow a path intermediate between a circular path and a cycloidal path. The action of the suspension spring itself does not produce any departure from equality in the times of vibration of the pendulum with varying arcs, as the force exerted by it on the pendulum at any instant is always proportional to the distance of the bob from its middle position. The stronger the spring, the longer the pendulum must be for the same rate of vibration, as the action of the spring is equivalent to increasing g in the pendulum formula. Sometimes a double strip of spring is employed for the suspension, one strip being arranged in front of the other and both being mounted between the same clamps or chops. It is of the greatest importance that the pendulum should be suspended from a rigid support.

In an interesting recent escapement due to Dr. Riefler of Munich, which has been used in observatories, the impulse to the pendulum is given through the suspension spring, which is bent through a certain angle each swing. As in a gravity escapement, the impulses are equal and do not vary with the driving force of the train. There are two escape wheels moving together on one axis, the front wheel being slightly larger than the other. The suspension spring is connected with the anchor which carries the pallets. The latter consist of two pins, the front portions of which are cut down to semicircles, and the flat surfaces serve as locking faces with which the front escape wheel engages. When the wheel is released from these faces, the back wheel engages with the complete portions of the pallet pins and, by turning the anchor through a small angle, slightly bends the suspension spring, thus supplying the necessary constant impulses to the pendulum.

For the purpose of regulation, the bob of a pendulum slides loosely on its rod and is supported by a nut below, which screws on to a thread on the end of the rod. By turning the nut in a right-handed direction, the bob is raised. This shortens the effective length of the pendulum and causes the clock to go faster, while unscrewing the nut has a contrary effect. A graduated scale is sometimes placed on the nut to indicate the effect which a certain rotation may be expected to produce. In high-class clocks, where it is not considered desirable to stop the pendulum for regulation, the clock is sometimes made to gain by adding small weights to a group of such weights placed on the top of the bob, which takes a cylindrical form. Similarly, weights can be removed to make the clock go slower.

The accurate timekeeping of a clock is affected by variations in the length of its pendulum with changes of temperature, and the methods of compensating for these changes are given in Chapter VII. Another source of error, of much less importance, however, arises from variations in the density of the air in which the pendulum swings.

The pendulum's motion is always opposed to some extent by the friction between it and the atmosphere, and, in addition, it continually does work in churning up the air in the clock case. When the barometer is high, this air is more dense and of greater weight, and this reduces the effective weight of the pendulum. If the latter be placed in a vacuum, the clock gains in comparison with its behaviour under ordinary conditions, and it is similarly affected, though to a less extent, by the continual variations in the barometer. The "barometric error" is not very great, being something like half a second a day for 1 in. change in the barometer, and it need only be compensated for in clocks aiming at a high standard of accuracy. The increase in the resistance of the atmosphere which accompanies a rise in the barometer would cause the clock to lose if the arc of swing of its pendulum remain constant, but this increased resistance also decreases the arc of swing; and this latter action, by reducing the circular error, tends to make the clock gain. These two opposite effects may possibly neutralize one another and, according to Lord Grimthorpe, this condition was realized in the Westminster clock. Generally,

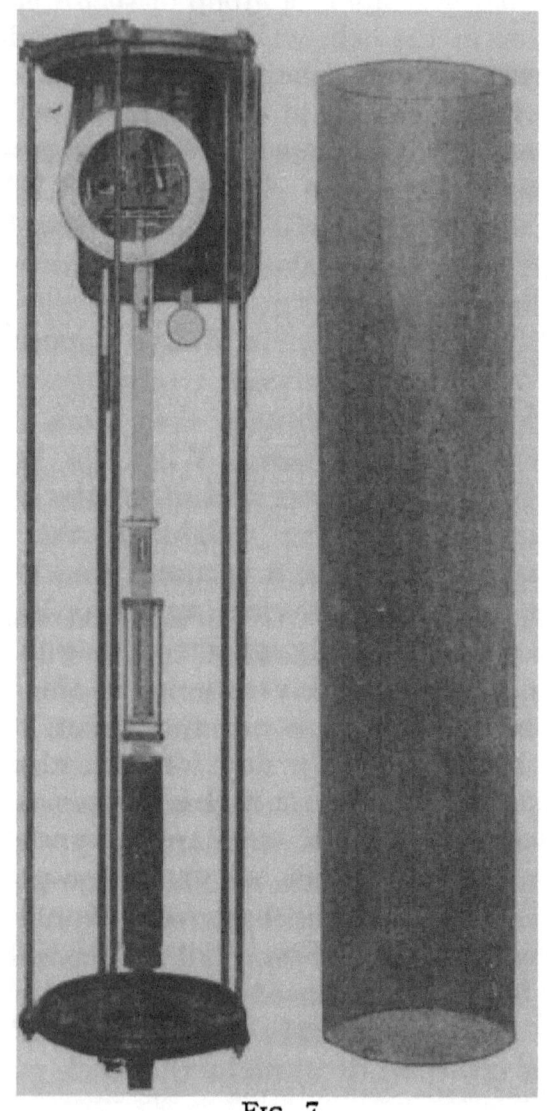

Fig. 7

however, the former action predominates, and the clock loses with increased barometric pressure.

Various methods have been used as barometric compensation. In one system, due to Sir George Airy, the mercury column of the short limb of a barometer is made to move a horseshoe magnet, so that, when the barometer rises, the magnet approaches the pendulum bob, which itself carries a pair of magnets. The increased attraction between the two sets of magnets when nearer together causes the clock to gain an amount equivalent to the loss brought about by the increased density of the air. Thin barometers have also been mounted on the pendulums, and the rise of mercury in the tubes used to give the necessary gaining compensation for the loss due to increased density.

In some of the best modern clocks, such as are used in astronomical observatories, the whole of the mechanism, including the pendulum, is contained in an air-tight glass case, and the pressure of the air inside can be varied by means of an air pump. A barometer is mounted within the case, and it is thus possible to maintain a uniform pressure and avoid the barometric errors. The clock can even be regulated by varying the internal air pressure.

Fig. 7 represents such a clock made by Messrs. Gent & Co. It is an electric clock, and the movement is bolted directly to the stone work of a building. The cylindrical glass case is shown detached.

CHAPTER IV

THE BALANCE SPRING AND WATCH ESCAPEMENTS

THE invention connected with watches that corresponds to the application of the pendulum for controlling clocks is the balance spring or "hairspring," which was introduced by Robert Hooke about 1660. It depends upon the principle, known as "Hooke's Law," that the extension or bending of a spring is proportional to the force acting upon it, provided the limit of elasticity of the material is not exceeded. In some of the earlier examples a straight spring was used, but this inconvenient form was replaced by a flat spiral. It was first applied to watches with verge escapements, and the foliot balance hitherto employed was transferred into a balanced wheel. The inner end of the spring was connected with the balance wheel and the outer end fixed. From Hooke's Law, it follows that the force due to the balance spring acting upon the balance at any instant is proportional to the angular distance of the balance from its mid-position, and it consequently follows that, if subject to the action of the spring only, the time of vibration of the balance would be independent of the angle of vibration. With the verge escapement, the balance, besides being under the action of the spring, is also subjected to the action of the escape wheel in assisting and retarding its motion. The controlling forces, however, include a factor which is independent of the driving force of the wheel train and which was absent from the old foliot balance arrangement, and much better timekeeping can be attained than was conceivable with the foliot balance.

THE BALANCE SPRING AND WATCH ESCAPEMENTS 41

Verge escapements were formerly very extensively employed, and the manufacture of verge watches was continued until well past the middle of the nineteenth century.

The horizontal or cylinder escapement was invented by George Graham in 1725, and is an improved form of an earlier escapement due to Tompion. The escape wheel teeth are pointed and engage with the surfaces of an incomplete cylinder CD (Fig. 8), upon which the balance is mounted. The impulses are given by the inclined face of a tooth, A, acting upon the edges C and D of the cylinder. A tooth is first locked by resting upon the outer surface of the cylinder ; but as the balance rotates, the tooth is freed and gives the impulse, resting during the remainder of the oscillation of the balance on the inner surface of the cylinder. During the next oscillation, the same tooth is freed and gives an impulse to the edge D of the cylinder, the wheel advancing until the next tooth is stopped by the outside of the cylinder. The edges or lips of the cylinder are rounded and the impulse surfaces of the wheel teeth have a convex form. During each oscillation, the wheel is giving an impulse to the cylinder through about 20° or more of the latter's motion, while at other times the wheel is in frictional contact with the cylinder.

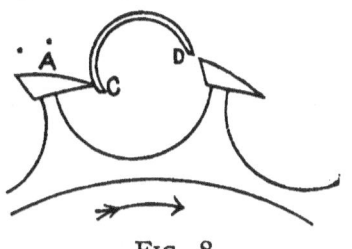

FIG. 8

On the rim of the balance there is a small projecting pin which, when there is no driving force acting on the watch, is diametrically opposite to a fixed stop with which the pin would engage should half the angle of swing of the balance reach an amount approaching to

180°. The pin and stop thus limit the motion of the balance, and prevent it rotating too far and producing a condition known as overbanking. As the balance may swing through an angle reaching up to about 180° from its middle position, it is not possible to have the teeth in the same plane as the escape wheel, and the teeth are consequently mounted on the ends of vertical arms projecting upward from the wheel itself. It is also necessary to cut away the cylinder to a greater extent below the acting portion.

In one form of this escapement, which was used by Breguet to a limited extent, the acting part of the cylinder overhangs below the bottom pivot of the balance wheel, and a simpler form of tooth was possible, though even then the wheel could not be arranged in one plane.

Graham and other English makers made watches in the eighteenth century with the horizontal escapement, the best of which had ruby cylinders. The escape wheels were of brass. The horizontal escapement has, however, been much more extensively and successfully used in Switzerland and France than in England. The foreign practice has generally been to use small steel wheels instead of the larger brass wheels formerly used in England. It is a much inferior escapement to the English lever, as the balance wheel is more under the control of the action of the wheel train.

The duplex escapement was introduced about 1775, and it is not clear by whom it was invented. On the arbor of the balance wheel there is a jewelled cylindrical piece with a notch, which is known as the ruby roller, and also a projecting finger serving as an impulse pallet. The escape wheel has two sets of teeth, one arranged horizontally in a plane perpendicular to the escape wheel axis, while the other set of teeth project upward. The horizontal set of teeth engage with the ruby roller and the vertical set with the impulse pallet. When the balance is rotating in one direction, the notch in the ruby roller allows the wheel to move forward, and one of the vertical teeth gives the impulse to the finger. On the return oscillation, the wheel is not freed, and the impulse is given on alternate beats only. Like the cylinder escapement, the duplex is of the frictional rest type, as when not giving an impulse, the wheel is always in contact with the moving ruby roller ; but as the latter is comparatively small and, moreover, a polished jewel, the friction is not so considerable as in the cylinder escapement. At one time, the duplex escapement was employed to a considerable extent for high-class watches, but it was found to be liable to miss an impulse if the watch received a jerk. It still survives, however, in the popular Waterbury watch.

The detached lever escapement is the best for pocket watches, and is the one now most commonly employed. It was invented by Thomas Mudge about the middle of the eighteenth century, but was not used to any extent until a much later date. The escape wheel teeth, shown in Fig. 9, engage with the jewelled pallets AB, which are mounted on an anchor carried by the lever CD. One end of this lever is notched to allow it to engage with a jewel pin P, which is secured to a disc R, known as a roller. The latter is fixed on the balance staff, which is the name for the axis of the balance wheel. Two pins, known as banking pins, limit the movement of the lever. An escape wheel tooth rests against the locking face of pallet A until the oscillation of the balance causes the roller pin to move the lever and release the tooth, which then engages with the impulse face of the pallet and, pushing it on one side, causes the lever to give an impulse to the roller pin. The locking face of the other pallet now intercepts the wheel, and another tooth rests on its locking face awaiting a repetition of the process, the wheel moving through a space of half a tooth each time. In this arrangement, the balance is altogether

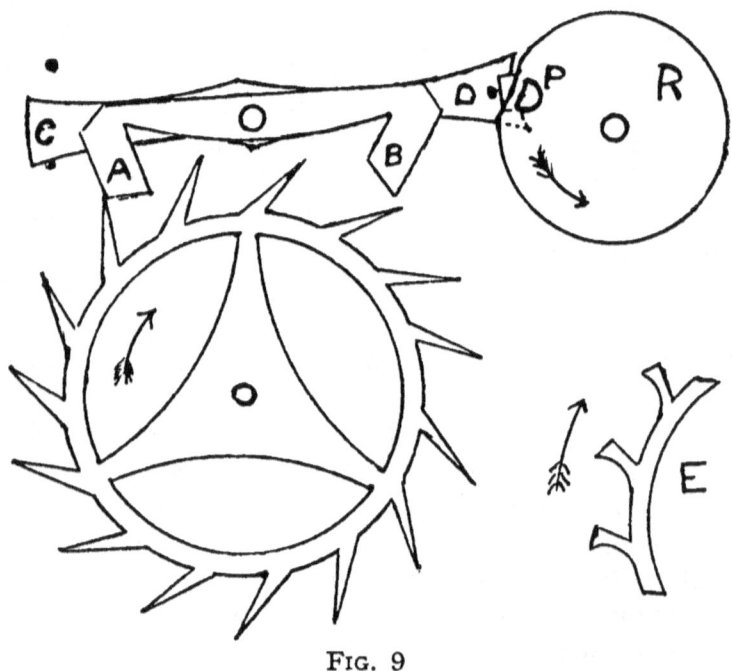

Fig. 9

free of the escapement during the greater part of its swing, that is, it is a "detached" escapement, and the impulse arcs correspond closely with the middle of the swing, both of which features are desirable from theoretical considerations.

The distance between the locking faces of the two pallets corresponds with $2\frac{1}{2}$ wheel teeth and, as there are 15 teeth in the wheel, this distance represents an angle of 60° ($2\frac{1}{2} \times \frac{360}{15}$) at the centre of the wheel.

If a wheel tooth engaged with the impulse face of one pallet until the exact instant that the tooth, next to come into action, engaged with the locking face of the other pallet, the impulse faces would project an angle equal to half a wheel tooth, that is 12°, at the centre of the wheel. In actual practice, it is necessary to make the impulse faces smaller than this; and the difference, during which the wheel is out of engagement with the pallets, is known as the " drop." The lever moves through an angle of about 10° each operation, of which about $1\frac{1}{2}°$ is occupied by unlocking and $8\frac{1}{2}°$ by the impulse.

Near to the notch in the lever there is a pin known as the safety pin, which serves to prevent the lever moving except when engaged by the roller pin. Otherwise, if the lever moved from one extreme position to the other, as it might do, if, say, the hands were moved backward, the roller pin on its return would not be able to engage with the notch of the lever, but would knock against the outside of the latter. Part of the roller is cut away to allow the safety pin to pass it when the lever moves.

The locking faces do not take the form of circles with the pallet staff as centre, as in the case of the deadbeat clock escapement, but are set at an angle, so that an escape wheel tooth, when engaging with one of the locking faces, tends to " draw " it towards the centre of the wheel. This keeps the lever against a banking pin and prevents the safety pin continually touching the roller.

In the club tooth lever escapement, the wheel teeth are shaped as shown at E in the figure. This form of tooth is well designed to retain the necessary oil, and a smaller angle of " drop " is possible than with the pointed teeth. It has long been used in Swiss and

American watches, and is now employed in less pretentious watches of English make.

In Swiss watches, the arbor of the escape wheel, the pallet staff, and the balance staff are placed in line ; an arrangement known as a straight-line escapement as distinguished from the right-angled escapement shown in Fig. 9, which was usually employed in English watches until recent times.

For high-class watches, a double roller escapement is employed, in which the safety pin is replaced by a finger ; and a second roller, smaller than the one on which the roller pin is mounted, is provided for the safety action only.

Mudge's early lever escapement was of the double-roller type, but his pallets had circular locking faces, and the connection between the lever and balance was unnecessarily complicated. It was a detached escapement ; and it seems strange that at a later date (1791) the much inferior rack-lever escapement was patented by Peter Litherland, of Liverpool, and was used in many watches. In this escapement, one end of the lever consisted of a toothed segment or rack, gearing with a pinion on the axis of the balance, which was consequently never free of the lever.

When fixing a balance or hair spring in position, the spring is passed through a small hole and secured by means of a tapered pin. The inner end is attached in this manner to a small split ring, or collet, of brass, which fits on the axis of the balance wheel, while the outer end of the spring is pinned to a stud which is attached to a fixed portion of the watch. At one time, in English watches it was usual permanently to mount the stud on the top plate of the watch, an arrangement which necessitated unpinning the spring every time that the balance wheel was removed and

THE BALANCE SPRING AND WATCH ESCAPEMENTS 47

adjusting it to its proper position when the balance wheel was replaced. It is now usual to attach the stud, either by a screw or by a tight fit, to the balance cock, which is the name of the piece which carries the upper bearing of the balance wheel. With this arrangement, the cock, wheel, and spring can be removed together without unpinning the spring.

The longer the spring, the slower the watch goes; while, on the contrary, if the spring be shortened, the watch will gain.

In ordinary pocket watches, regulation is obtained by altering the effective length of the balance spring. Near to the fixed end of the spring there are two pins close together, between which the spring passes. These are known as curb pins, and are mounted on a piece named the regulator, which can be moved with the axis of the balance wheel as its centre. When the balance wheel rotates in a direction which coils up the spring, the portion between the curb pins comes into contact with the inner pin before the balance reaches its extreme position; and during the return swing, when the coils open out, the spring similarly comes into contact with the other pin. During the portions of the balance's motion, while the spring is in contact with either pin, the effective length of the spring is reduced approximately by the amount between the pins and the fixed end, and consequently the watch goes faster than it would do if there were no curb pins to restrict the motion sideways of the spring. It will thus be seen that the greater the distance between the fixed end of the spring and the curb pins, the greater will be the reduction of the effective length of the spring and the faster the watch will go.

To obtain this result, the regulator is moved away from the fixed end towards the letter F, which is generally engraved on the watch; movement of the regulator in the opposite direction, that is, towards the letter S, causes the watch to lose. In some old verge watches the letters F and S are replaced by engraved figures of a hare and a snail, while in Swiss watches the symbols A and R are used.

The closer the curb pins are to one another, the more the effective shortening of the spring will be; and sometimes when the required change in the rate of the watch cannot be obtained by moving the regulator to its extreme position, the necessary adjustment can be obtained by opening or closing the pins. The proper method in such a case, however, is to alter the fixed end of the spring, unless the change required is very small. Sometimes it happens, generally after the watch has been badly shaken, that an additional coil of the spring gets between the curb pins and causes the watch to gain considerably. In fact, when a watch gains at an alarming rate, it is well to suspect that this is the cause. Some watches have the end of the inner pin bent outwards to form with the outer pin a closed loop, into which an additional coil cannot be displaced.

It is necessary that the spring should be so adjusted that when the balance wheel is in the mean position between the two impulses, which it receives from the escapement, the spring is in the neutral position where it does not exert any influence on the balance in either direction. In lever watches this is tested by "blocking" the wheel train, that is, inserting a thin piece of wire in the way of one of the arms of a wheel, so that the train is stopped. The balance wheel then comes to rest with the hairspring in its neutral position and, if the adjustment is correct, the lever will at the same time be halfway between the banking pins.

THE BALANCE SPRING AND WATCH ESCAPEMENTS 49

It is not strictly true that the time of vibràtion of a balance wheel controlled by a hairspring is the same whether the arc of vibration is large or small, as the action is complicated, being influenced by the moving weight of the spring itself. For each spring, however, there is a length for which this condition, known as isochronism, closely applies ; but when this length has been determined, it is not possible to maintain isochronism if the watch is regulated by varying the length of the spring. For this reason, better class watches and ships' chronometers are not regulated by altering the length of the spring, but by means of timing screws on the rim of the balance wheel. If the watch gains, these screws are unscrewed a little, thus moving their slight weights to a greater distance from the centre of the balance and consequently causing the watch to go slower. In ships' chronometers there are two screws at the extremities of the diametral arm of the compensation balance : but in watches which, unlike a ship's chronometer, are placed at various times in different positions, additional timing screws are provided. Usually there are four occupying positions at right angles to one another. Both forms of balance are illustrated on page 79.

When a watch is placed on a flat surface with the axis of its balance wheel vertical, the friction opposing the motion of the balance wheel is almost entirely that on the lower end of the balance pivot ; but when the watch is placed vertical, the friction is on the sides of the pivots. In the latter case, the friction is greater than when the watch lies flat, and the arc of vibration is consequently less. In adjusting watches, which are required to keep accurate time, it is necessary to arrange that the time occupied by the long arcs and the short arcs shall be equal. With ships' chronometers, it is arranged that the timekeeper shall occupy the horizontal position all the time. The case of the movement has two bearings opposite to one another in a brass ring, which is itself mounted on two similar bearings in a fixed outer box, the second pair of bearings being at right angles to those first mentioned. As a result, if the outer box is inclined in any direction, it is possible for the movement to swing upon the two bearings or "gimbals," so that it retains a practically horizontal position.

In action, the flat spiral balance usually employed in ordinary pocket watches does not open out and close up its coils symmetrically about the centre, and this leads to a varying side friction on the balance wheel pivots. Chronometers employ helical or cylindrical spiral springs in which this defect is absent, while in modern pocket watches a form intermediate between the flat and the cylindrical spiral is used. This consists of the "overcoil" or Breguet spring, in which the outer coil is bent upwards and inwards towards the centre, the fixed end of the spring being much nearer the centre than the outside coil. The regulator pins embrace a portion of the overcoil. With this arrangement, a more symmetrical action of the spring is obtained, and there is less side friction on the pivots than with the flat form of spring.

In the trials of watches which were formerly conducted at Kew, but are now carried out at the National Physical Observatory, Teddington, the tests include the determination of the watch's daily rate with the pendant uppermost, pendant to the right, and pendant to the left. To eliminate small positional errors of the escapement, which would thus be revealed, an interesting device due to Breguet and known as the tourbillon, is sometimes employed. In this, the escapement is mounted on a carriage, which revolves continuously round the fourth wheel as centre and occupies all the successive vertical positions once each minute.

The karrusel is another device of the same type, in which, however, the carriage revolves about once an hour.

CHAPTER V

GENERAL MECHANISMS

THE escapement which, as we have seen, controls the timekeeping of the clock, is kept in action by a driving weight or spring, and the series of wheels transmitting the motion is known as the wheel train. There are various arrangements of wheel trains, but the following may be taken as typical of an English weight-driven clock, with a pendulum beating seconds and designed to go eight days for each winding.

Fig. 10 represents the arrangement; but for simplicity, the wheels and pinions are shown as circles only, the teeth being omitted.

The weight W is suspended by means of a pulley round which a cord passes. One end of the cord, A, is fixed to the framework of the clock, and the cord passes round and round a drum or barrel, to which it is secured at the other end. The great wheel GW', or first wheel of the train, is concentric with the barrel, but is not rigidly connected with it, as it is necessary to provide for the winding-up of the weight. Secured to the barrel there is a ratchet wheel R, engaging with a click, C, which is mounted on the great wheel. On the end of the arbor of the barrel there is a square over which the winding key fits. On turning this key in a right-handed or clockwise direction, more of the cord is wound on to the barrel and the weight is raised. The inclined faces of the ratchet wheel push the click away, and the latter does not oppose motion in this direction. Each time a tooth of the ratchet passes the click, the latter is pushed by its spring S towards the centre of the wheel, causing the succession of clicking noises which are heard as the clock is wound. If, however, any attempt were made to wind the barrel in a left-handed direction, the short radial faces of the ratchet would soon butt against the end of the click in such a manner as to prevent motion in that direction.

When the clock has been wound up, the action of the weight urges the ratchet against the click in the same manner, and this tends to cause the great wheel on which the click is mounted to rotate in a left-handed direction. The great wheel, to which we will assign 96 teeth, gears with an eight-toothed pinion on the centre wheel. (Pinions are toothed wheels with comparatively few teeth.) The centre wheel carries the minute hand, and must consequently rotate once an hour. It has 64 teeth, and engages with a pinion of 8 teeth on the third wheel of the train.

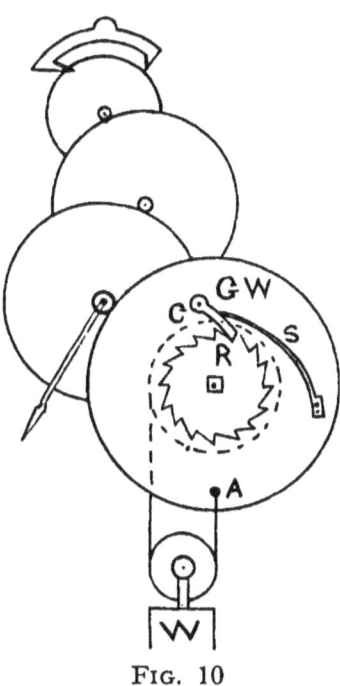

FIG. 10

This, in turn, has 60 teeth and gears, with a pinion of 8 teeth on the escape wheel. As the pendulum beats seconds and the escape wheel moves through the space of half a tooth each beat, this wheel must have 30 teeth if it is to rotate once a minute, an arrangement which is usually adopted with clocks provided with seconds pendulums, and a seconds hand can then be mounted on the escape wheel. In such cases, it is a necessary condition for correct working that the numbers of the teeth in the respective wheels and pinions shall be such that the escape wheel shall make sixty rotations for each rotation of the centre wheel.

The "value" of a train of wheel, or the ratio of the numbers of turns made in the same time by the last and first members of that train, is obtained by multiplying together the numbers of teeth in the driving wheels and dividing the product by the numbers of teeth in the followers (in this case, the pinions) also multiplied together. With the numbers of teeth taken in the example given, this value between the centre wheel and the escape wheel is—

$$\frac{\text{No. of teeth in centre wheel} \times \text{no. of teeth in 3rd wheel}}{\text{No. of teeth in 3rd pinion} \times \text{no. of teeth in escape-wheel pinion}}$$
or $\frac{64 \times 60}{8 \times 8} = 60$, which satisfies the conditions required.

As the centre wheel pinion has 8 teeth and the great wheel 96 teeth, the latter rotates once in $\frac{96}{8} = 12$ hrs.; and if the diameter of the barrel is 2 ins., the cord will be unwound $\frac{22}{7} \times 2$, or about 6·28 ins. in the same time. As the cord is double, the weight falls through only half the distance the cord unwinds from the barrel, that is, 3·14 ins. in 12 hrs., which is equivalent to a total fall of about 4 ft. 2 ins. in eight days. It is clear that to allow the clock to go for this period, it is necessary that, when fully wound, there should be at least 16 coils of cord round the barrel.

Many variations in the numbers of the teeth of both wheels and pinions are found, and the example given must be taken as typical only. Modifications of the numbers would be required, for example, if the pendulum did not beat seconds, and this is usually the case. Clocks of the better class, known as regulators, usually employ 12 teeth in the pinions. This leads to greater expense and also to more satisfactory working.

Satisfactory results cannot be obtained for transmitting the driving force if pinions of less than 7 or 8 teeth are used, and better results are obtained with ten or twelve. Sometimes, however, as low a number as six are used in the pinions of the subsidiary motion work driving the hands. In Harrison's chronometer, with which he obtained the award of £20,000 (*see* p. 84), as many as 21 teeth were used on the centre wheel pinion, but there is no advantage in employing such a large number.

The minute hand is not rigidly secured to the centre wheel, as it is necessary to provide for the hands to be moved independently of the main train of wheels. It is mounted on a piece known as a cannon pinion or wheel, which has a long boss fitting loosely on an extension of the centre wheel arbor. (In clock and watch work, axles are known as arbors.) Behind the cannon is a bent strip spring, having a square hole at the middle, which fits a correspondingly shaped portion of the arbor ; while in front of the hand there is a washer, and the hand is secured by a pin passing through a hole in the centre wheel arbor. The action of the spring ensures that the hand moves with the centre wheel, but, nevertheless, allows of an independent rotation when necessary. Gearing with the cannon, there is a wheel known as the minute wheel, which usually in striking clocks has the same number of teeth ; both, for example, may have 36 teeth. This wheel has a pinion of, say, 6 teeth gearing with the hour-wheel of 72 teeth, which is mounted on a pipe fitting loosely on a bridge-piece surrounding the cannon pinion. The hour-wheel carries the hour hand.

While winding up a clock, the weight of the latter ceases to be applied to driving the clock train and the clock would consequently lose time, unless some special provision were made. For this purpose, a maintaining power mechanism is provided, which was invented by John Harrison about 1750. This consists of a subsidiary driving spring, which is able to drive the clock for a short time. The driving force applied is less than that obtained from the normal driving weight, and the subsidiary spring is always kept wound up by the weight when the latter is in action.

The trains used in watches differ from those of clocks, as watches are generally arranged to go for 30 hours only with one winding, and their escape wheels are too small to allow of as many teeth as can conveniently be employed in clocks. Their balance wheels also vibrate more frequently than the pendulums of clocks. It is necessary to introduce an additional wheel into the train, which consists of a great wheel; a centre wheel carrying the minute hand; a third wheel; a fourth wheel, on which the seconds hand is mounted; and the escape wheel with 15 teeth. In lever watches, the balance usually makes $4\frac{1}{2}$ or 5 single vibrations in a second; but with cylinder escapements, five beats a second is the rule.

In a fusee watch, the great wheel is connected with the fusee by a ratchet wheel and clicks, two clicks being employed for safety instead of the one described for a clock train. A chain is secured to the fusee at one end and to the barrel at the other; and in the process of winding, three or more turns of the chain are unwound from the barrel, which contains the driving or main spring. This process involves rotating the fusee four or more times in a counter-clockwise direction. A maintaining power mechanism is provided, the click or detent for which is external to the fusee, and occupies a conspicuous position. The barrel arbor is kept stationary by means of a ratchet wheel engaging with a fixed click mounted on the bottom plate of the watch underneath the dial, and the mainspring is so designed that more turns of the barrel would be required to wind it up fully than are necessary for it to drive the fusee and great wheel for a period of 30 hours. The excess is used, in part, to set up the spring, so that there is a tension acting upon the chain even when the watch is run down. This ensures a driving force to the end of the action, and also keeps the chain taut. Part of the excess is to spare when the watch is fully wound up, and the mainspring is consequently never strained to its full extent and, moreover, the chain does not experience a pull beyond its strength.

It is necessary to provide a means of preventing overwinding, and this is achieved by a snail-shaped piece at the top of the fusee. As the chain rises up the fusee, it lifts a lever in opposition to the action of a spring; and when the chain reaches the last turn of the fusee, this lever has been so far raised that the point of the snail comes into contact with it, and is thus prevented from rotating further.

The chains used in watches are of a special type, and are built up of a number of flat pieces joined together in such a manner that the links of the chain consist alternately of two pieces and one piece. These pieces stand on their edges on the barrel.

In a going barrel watch, there is no fusee. The spring is arranged in the barrel as before, but the latter is made in one piece with the great wheel. To wind up the watch, the barrel arbor is rotated in the clockwise direction, the return motion of the arbor being prevented by a ratchet and click provided with a spring. As the force applied to wind up the mainspring is applied in the same direction as that in which the spring acts on the train, there is no need for a maintaining power mechanism.

To prevent overwinding in going-barrel watches, the Geneva stop has been extensively used. This is shown in Fig. 11. It consists of a piece A with one tooth, C, which is mounted on the end of the barrel arbor and engages with a star wheel B. The latter moves through one-fifth of a rotation for each turn of A; but when the convex portion D comes into contact with A, further rotation of the latter is impossible. It will be seen that this arrangement limits the movement of A to four turns. The mainspring itself is, in such cases, usually designed to permit of about five and a half to six turns, thus allowing of a margin for setting up the spring when the watch is run down, and leaving something to spare when the watch is fully wound up. By using only the middle portion of the spring's action, the extreme high and low tensions are eliminated, and the stop mechanism thus serves a double purpose.

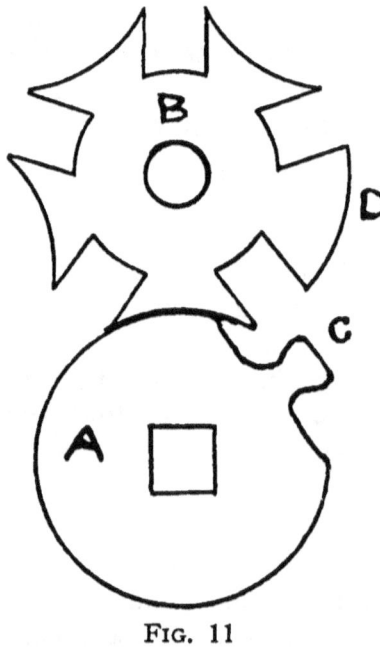

Fig. 11

In recent going-barrel watches, apart from the Geneva type, stop-work mechanisms are not usually provided, and the accuracy of the escapement is trusted to prevent errors due to variations in the driving force. As a matter of fact, for the requirements of ordinary pocket watches, it is not very serious if a watch does gain a little during the first portion of its run, provided it is wound up regularly every twenty-four hours and there is no accumulation of error during that period.

The wheel trains of watches are arranged between plates, which are provided with holes for the pivots. Pillars are attached to the bottom plate, and the top plate fits the ends of these pillars, being secured by screws or by pins. The bottom plate, which also carries the dial, consists of a whole circle, as does the top plate in a "full plate" watch, except for a gap for the barrel. In this case, the balance wheel is above the top plate, an arrangement which was usual in English watches until recent years. At the present time, a three-quarter plate is the usual practice, in which the train is so arranged that there is room to place the upper pivot of the balance in the same plane as the upper pivots of the other wheels. A narrower and more convenient movement is thus obtained. In some Geneva watches a bar movement is employed, in which a separate bar, screwed to the bottom plate and kept in position by two steady pins, is provided for each top pivot.

In the motion work or hand gearing of watches, the cannon pinion fits friction tight on the centre wheel arbor and gears with the so-called minute wheel, the pinion of which engages the hour-wheel. The minute wheel turns on a fixed pin and the hour-wheel fits loosely over the cannon pinion. A typical arrangement is a cannon pinion of 12 teeth, a minute wheel and pinion of 36 and 10 teeth respectively, and an hour wheel of 40 teeth. As $\frac{12 \times 10}{36 \times 40} = \frac{1}{12}$ the necessary ratio is thus obtained. In Geneva watches and in some three-quarter plate watches, the centre wheel arbor is made hollow, and the cannon pinion is fixed to a set square, consisting of a tapered piece, passing through the hollow. The operation of setting the hands to time is then effected from the back of the watch.

Stop watches are used for measuring short intervals of time, such as those occupied by athletes in running over certain distances. In one form, formerly extensively used, there is a sliding piece at the side of the case, which can be moved within certain limits. In one extreme position, a bent pin with a thin end touches the roller of the balance and stops the watch ; but when the sliding piece is at its uppermost position, the balance is free. The application, by means of the pin, of pressure upon the balance wheel is obviously an undesirable method of achieving the purpose in view, and better forms are now employed in which the main train of wheels and the balance are not interrupted. An additional train is employed, which is thrown in and out of action ; and an arrangement is provided by which the seconds hand is returned to the zero position before the commencement of each measurement. Watches of this class beat five times a second, and employ what is known as an 18,000 train, the number indicating the beats in an hour.

In centre-seconds watches, the seconds hand is mounted in the middle of the dial, an arrangement usually followed in the stop watches and chronographs just referred to. As the fourth wheel occupies the central position, the second wheel of the train is no longer a centre wheel, and special motion work is required for the hands. The extension of the fourth wheel arbor, upon which the seconds hand is fixed, passes through a pipe-shaped piece which is attached to the bottom plate, and the cannon wheel fits loosely over this pipe. The cannon wheel ; the minute wheel ; and an additional wheel, which is secured to a set square passing through a hollow second wheel arbor, have equal numbers of teeth ; while the hour wheel has twelve times as many teeth as the minute wheel pinion.

Until recent times, watches, like clocks, were usually wound up by means of a key with a hollow square, which engaged with a square on the fusee or the barrel arbor ; while the hands were similarly set to time by means of a square on the cannon pinion. Such an arrangement is unsuual in a watch of recent construction, and provision is now made for winding up the mainspring and setting the hands without opening the case or using any appliance not included in the watch itself. The operations are effected by a milled knob or button fitting over the pendant at the top of the case.

The earliest keyless watches now appear to be somewhat freakish in their design, but they date back to the seventeenth century. About 1755, Pierre A. Caron made a watch for Madame de Pompadour, which was wound up by means of a piece projecting from the side of the case, the piece being partially turned around the edge of the case to wind up the watch. Caron afterwards became the famous librettist Beaumarchais. Some of the early keyless mechanism had " pumping " actions, in which the mainspring was wound up by means of a piece at the pendant, which was pushed down and pulled up several times.

Napoleon I had a watch of a type described as self-winding, in which a weighted lever, supported by a spring, rises and falls for every step taken by the wearer when walking. By means of a pawl and ratchet, it was arranged that this vibratory motion should wind up the watch. A similar mechanism has been employed in the appliances known as pedometers, for determining the distance a person walks. The mechanism records the total number of steps taken, and adjustments, corresponding with the average length of the step taken by the wearer, must be made before the instrument can be used.

In another form of self-winding mechanism for use with hunter cases, the opening and closing of the case,

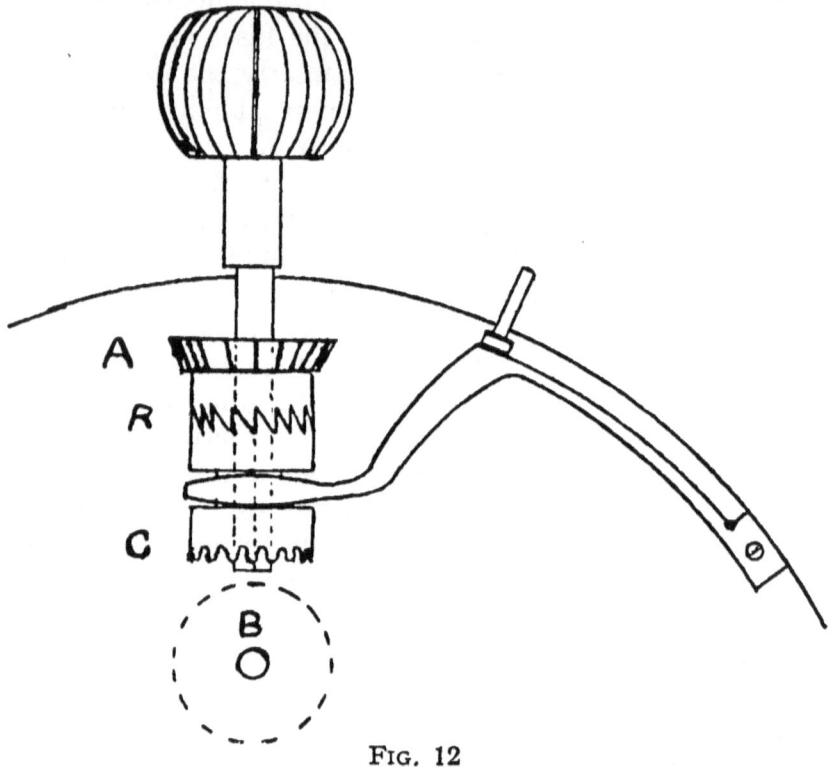

Fig. 12

necessary to see the time, was arranged to wind up the mainspring.

In 1820, T. Prest patented a keyless device in which a rotating button in the pendant was employed for the same purpose.

Fig. 12 represents a keyless mechanism which has been used to a considerable extent in Swiss and other watches, and which is of a type introduced about the middle of the nineteenth century. Two ratchet wheels, with their teeth on the ends of cylinders (or contrate ratchet wheels), are employed, one of which drives the other. For motion in one direction, the two sets of teeth interlock and the wheels move together; but when the driver is turned in the opposite direction, the teeth slide out of contact. The driver forms part of a sliding piece RC fitting on a square at the lower end of the stem of the winding button, and RC is urged upward by a spring into engagement with the other contrate ratchet, which fits loosely on the circular part of the button stem and is attached to a pinion A. The latter gears with a wheel, not shown, which is connected with the barrel arbor and winds up the watch, a click and spring being provided. When the button is rotated in a right-hand direction, RC moves with it; and, from the shape of the teeth, it is obvious that it will carry A with it and so wind up the mainspring. A motion of the button in the opposite direction simply results in the teeth of RC slipping over those of the other contrate ratchet, and produces no winding effect. To set the hands, RC is depressed by means of a push piece, which acts upon an attachment to the spring that normally urges RC upward. Another contrate wheel C then engages with a spur wheel B, which is in gear with the minute wheel of the motion work, the winding gear being out of action during this process.

An alternative type of keyless mechanism, which is usually employed in English watches, is the rocking-bar mechanism, which was invented by Gustavus Huguenin in 1855. The button carries either a bevel or a contrate wheel, which engages with a second wheel, the bearing of which serves as a centre for a bar upon which two other wheels, which we will call A and B, are mounted. Both of these wheels engage with the second wheel, and a spring so acts upon the bar that it tends to keep A in contact with a winding wheel attached to the barrel arbor. Motion of the button in one direction winds up the spring, while a reverse motion causes A to slip in and out of contact with the winding wheel, the bar rocking backwards and forwards during the process. To set the hands, the bar is acted upon by depressing a push piece, which throws A out of action and brings the wheel B into engagement with the motion wheels connected with the hands.

In some recent keyless watches, the use of a push piece for setting the hands is dispensed with, and automatic connection between the button and the motion work obtained by raising the former a short distance in the pendant.

Jewelled bearings for watch work were introduced about the end of the seventeenth century by Nicholas Faccio, and are now universally employed for the balance-wheel pivots, the roller pin, and the pallet surfaces. In addition, they are frequently employed for the smaller wheels of the train. They have the advantage of reducing the friction, and the jewelled surfaces are not subject to corrosion by the oil. For the balance wheel, there are two jewels, with holes through which the pivots pass; while, in addition, there are two flat jewelled surfaces with which the ends of the pivots are in contact. These flat jewels are known as end stones, and in better class watches are often provided for the pallet staff and the escape-wheel pivots, in addition to the balance staff. When a watch is described as "jewelled in 15 actions," it generally indicates that there are the two jewel holes and the two end stones for the balance, one jewel for the roller pin, two for the pallets faces and two for the pallet staff pivots, two for the escape-wheel bearings, two for the fourth wheel, and two for the third wheel, making a total of fifteen.

The acting pallet surfaces of clocks often take the form of jewels, which are also sometimes used for the escape wheel and the pallet bearings in high-class clocks. In some French clocks, the pallets consist of jewel pins, and these escapements are arranged so that the escape wheel is in front of the dial and the action of the escapement visible.

One method of reducing the friction, which has been extensively used in scientific instruments, is the employment of friction wheels. This method has not been used to any extent in clocks; but in the Science Museum there is an exceptional example, in which friction wheels were employed by Benjamin Vulliamy in a clock made for King George III. This clock was the principal timekeeper in His Majesty's private observatory at Kew, and was afterwards the property of George IV and William IV. Each pivot rests upon a pair of wheels, which move through a much smaller angle than that through which the pivot rotates, with the result that there is a reduction in the friction. The wheels supporting the bearings for the pallets are arranged symmetrically below the axis; but for the other bearings of the train, one of each set of friction wheels is placed partly to the side of the pivot, in accordance with the direction in which the pressure of the pivot acts. An arrangement is provided whereby the great wheel can be lifted from its delicate bearing during winding.

Henry Sully, a famous horologist, who settled in France, used friction wheels in a chronometer constructed in 1724; and they were also employed by Harrison and Mudge.

CHAPTER VI

STRIKING MECHANISMS

DIFFERENT arrangements have been provided for causing clocks to indicate the successive hours by striking upon a bell or gong ; but the only two methods which have been used to any considerable extent are the locking plate and the rack-striking mechanisms, although the details of each of these have been subjected to various modifications.

The locking-plate mechanism is found in the earliest clocks from the fourteenth century onwards, and is still used, with improvements, in modern turret clocks. In both systems there is a train of wheels, which is driven independently of the " going " or timekeeping train by a separate weight or spring, and includes a wheel known as the pin wheel, upon which a series of equidistant pins are mounted. These pins engage with the tail of a lever carrying a hammer, which strikes the bell, the return motion of the hammer being obtained from a spring. The pin wheel is (generally) the second wheel in the striking train. A pin on the minute wheel of the clock, which rotates once an hour, engages with a lever and brings the striking mechanism into operation. This lever forms one of a system of levers or arms, and its first action is to release the train by disengaging a stop which normally locks the third wheel of the train. The latter is then free to move under the action of the driving weight, but it is soon brought to rest by the action of another stop, which now engages with a pin on the fourth wheel of the train, known as the warning wheel. This preliminary motion is known as the " warning," and can usually be noticed a short time before a clock begins to strike. The various arms continue to be raised until the operating pin on the minute wheel passes completely out of contact with the lever with which it engages ; then the arms all fall, the fourth wheel is no longer locked, and the train is free to move.

The position of a piece known as the locking plate decides how long the freedom of the train continues and how many times the pin wheel causes the hammer to strike the bell or gong. The locking plate consists of a disc with a number of slots in its circumference (*see* Fig. 13), and it is connected with the train. While a hook connected with the system of levers is in contact with the circumference of the disc, the train remains free ; but when the locking plate has moved round with the train into such a position that the hook is above one of the slots, the hook falls into that slot and causes a stop on a lever, which moves with it, to lock the third wheel of the train, which then remains at rest until a repetition of the process occurs in an hour's time.

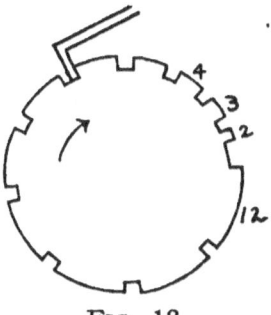

Fig. 13

The distance between the successive slots on the locking wheel are proportional to 2, 3, 4, etc., up to 12. For 1 o'clock, there is simply an enlarged slot, as no action of the locking plate is required at this hour.

Similarly, by increasing all the slots, the clock can be made to strike 1 every alternate operation ; and by placing two pins diametrically opposite to one another on the minute wheel, it can then be arranged that the clock strikes the half-hours as well as the hours.

The method of indicating the half-hour by striking 1 is not altogether satisfactory, and does not impart much information when heard in the middle of the night. One system used in some Dutch clocks is to employ two bells, on one of which the hours are struck, while the half-hours are indicated by an equal number of strokes on the second bell, which emits a different sound.

It is obvious that if a clock with a locking-plate mechanism stops, it is necessary, when setting it to time, to wait at each hour for the full number of strokes to be struck, as the number of strokes at any hour does not depend directly upon the time indicated by the clock. The rack-striking mechanism, which was invented by the Rev. E. Barlow in 1676, is free from this objection, as, with it, the number of strokes is determined by a flat spiral, or snail (*see* Fig. 14), which moves with the hand work, sometimes, in fact, being mounted upon the wheel carrying the hour hand. It appears to have been first introduced as a means of making clocks strike the number of hours indicating the time, whenever desired, an operation known as repeating.

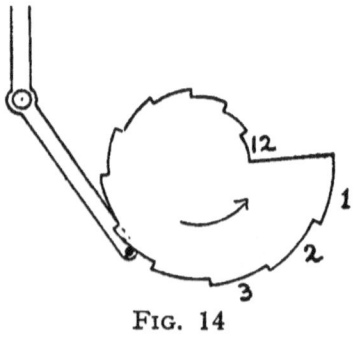

Fig. 14

An essential feature of the mechanism is a rack with pointed teeth, which is mounted on a piece carrying an arm or tail, the latter being urged against the snail by a spring. Normally, this piece is kept away from the snail by means of a large click or rack hook, which engages with the extreme left teeth of the rack, while at the same time the striking train is locked by a piece on the arbor of the third wheel being in

STRIKING MECHANISMS

contact with a pin mounted on the rack. This piece is known as the gathering pallet, and, in addition to its "tail," which effects the locking, it has a tooth which is situated opposite to the tail and engages with the teeth of the rack when the third wheel rotates. The gathering pallet and the rack are situated in front of the plates in which the main wheels are mounted, the third wheel arbor being prolonged through its bearing to permit of this arrangement. As in the locking-plate mechanism, there is a double arm or lifting piece which is actuated by a pin on one of the hand-work wheels, generally the minute wheel, rotating once an hour. When raised, this lifting piece moves the rack hook out of contact with the rack, and the latter is now free to move to the left under the action of its spring, until its tail comes into contact with the snail, as shown in the figure. The gathering pallet no longer engages with the pin on the rack, and the striking train consequently moves until a pin on its fourth wheel meets a stop on the lifting piece, the end of which passes through a slot in the plate. This is the warning action as described in connection with the locking-plate mechanism. When the pin actuating the lifting piece moves out of contact with it, the lifting piece falls, and the fourth wheel is no longer stopped. The striking train is now again free and continues in motion during the striking of the hours. The second wheel of the train carries a series of pins, which engage with the hammer striking the bell; and the third wheel, which rotates once for each stroke, carries the gathering pallet, the tooth of which moves the rack through the space of one tooth during the same time. When all the teeth of the rack have been gathered up, the tail of the gathering pallet again comes into contact with the pin mounted on the rack, and the train is again locked. The number of strokes each operation is thus determined by the amount to which the rack moved to the left, and this amount was clearly decided by the position of the snail. Instead of taking the form of a continuous spiral, the snail is usually arranged in steps.

To strike the half hours, an additional pin is provided on the minute wheel, but this pin is so arranged that it does not raise the lifting piece to the same extent as it is raised before striking the hours. The first tooth of the rack, that is, the extreme left-hand one, is made shorter than the others ; and at the half-hours the rack hook is raised sufficiently to allow this one tooth to escape past it while retaining the second tooth, with the result that the clock strikes 1 only.

Except for turret clocks, the rack-striking mechanism is now generally preferred to the locking plate. In both systems, the striking train ends in a fly or two-bladed fan, which moves in opposition to the resistance of the air and regulates the rate at which the blows are struck.

When the hands are put back, in one of the arrangements employed, the motion work pin engages with the underside of the lifting piece, which is twisted somewhat to allow of this ; and the action of the pin is to push the lifting piece to one side until the pin passes clear of it. The lifting piece takes the form of a strip thin enough to permit of its being sprung aside in this manner.

Watches which are made to strike the hours in a similar manner to a clock are known as clock-watches, and many of this type were formerly made. The introduction of the rack striking mechanism, however, rendered possible the introduction of an important class of watches known as repeaters, which, before the introduction of matches, were much more extensively used than at present. Either by pushing a button at the crown of a watch, or by sliding a piece at the side, it was possible to make the watch strike the hour at any time and any number of times. The rack and snail mechanism was the principal feature; and when pushing the button, the necessary work was done for winding up a separate spring which drove the striking train. Repeaters were made which merely indicated the hours; while others gave the quarters and half-quarters and, in some, even the minutes past the quarters were struck. Sometimes bells were used and, in others, wire gongs; while in one type, known as dumb repeaters, only a knock of the hammer in the case was heard. In the earlier types, if the operating button were not completely pushed home, it was possible for too few a number of hours to be struck. To obviate this disadvantage, a device known as the "all-or-nothing" piece was introduced by Julien Le Roy. This ensured that the repeater either indicated the hours completely or not at all. As has been previously stated, the rack mechanism was invented by the Rev. E. Barlow, but improvements in its application to repeaters are due to Daniel Quare. Repeating clocks were made about 1676, and the mechanism was applied to watches about ten years later.

Alarm clocks were introduced in the early days of clock-making, when, it is said, the bells simply striking the hours could not always be relied upon to wake the priests in the monasteries for prayers in the middle of the night. In various modifications which have been used, there is a separate train of wheels driving an escapement, in which a hammer is mounted on the pallets. A common arrangement consists of a spring-driven train, with an anchor escapement carrying a hammer, which strikes the bell. Attached to the hammer there is a tail piece, which normally is in contact with a disc on an adjustable piece fitting on the hour-wheel. This disc prevents any motion of the hammer; but it is notched, and when, in the course of time, the tail-piece is opposite the notch, the hammer is free to move and is set in vibration by the escapement, thus causing the bell to ring continuously. By adjusting the position of the disc in relation to the hour-wheel, the time at which the release occurs can be varied as required.

CHAPTER VII

TEMPERATURE COMPENSATION

MOST bodies expand when heated and contract when cooled, and this causes clocks with pendulums, including metal rods, to lose in hot weather and to gain in cold weather, unless special provisions are made to counteract the variation in length of the pendulum rod. In 1726, Graham introduced the mercurial compensation pendulum, which, until recent years, was extensively used in the construction of clocks of the better class, as well as in others not answering that description. The pendulum bob consists of a jar of mercury; and as with any increase of temperature the column of mercury will increase its length to a greater proportional extent than the steel pendulum rod, it is possible so to proportion the various parts that any change of temperature will not affect the position of the centre of oscillation of the pendulum.

There have been several modifications of Graham's pendulum. In one form, two jars are mounted side by side; while in another, the pendulum rod takes the form of a tube, and contains mercury for the greater part of its length.

From Graham's account of his invention, published in the *Philosophical Transactions*, it appears that he was experimenting with mercury as a possible material for a levelling instrument, and came to the conclusion that it was unsuitable for that purpose. He, however, noticed that the volume of mercury increased to a large extent comparatively when it was near a fire. Previously he had attempted to construct a compensation pendulum, the action of which depended upon the different expansions of two metals, and had decided that the differences were not sufficient to render his scheme practicable. His observation of the expanding mercury, however, gave him a clue as to another method of attacking the problem.

About the same time, John Harrison successfully designed a compensation pendulum depending upon the different expansions of two metals. This is known as the gridiron pendulum, and was formerly extensively used.

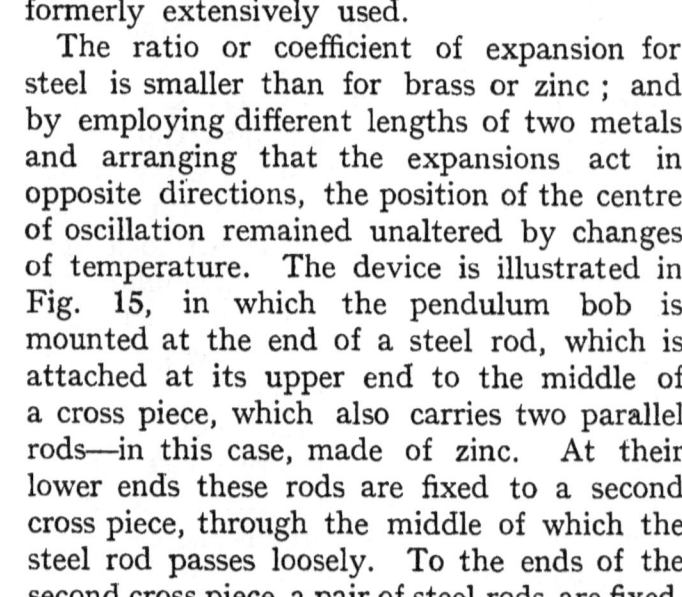

FIG. 15

The ratio or coefficient of expansion for steel is smaller than for brass or zinc; and by employing different lengths of two metals and arranging that the expansions act in opposite directions, the position of the centre of oscillation remained unaltered by changes of temperature. The device is illustrated in Fig. 15, in which the pendulum bob is mounted at the end of a steel rod, which is attached at its upper end to the middle of a cross piece, which also carries two parallel rods—in this case, made of zinc. At their lower ends these rods are fixed to a second cross piece, through the middle of which the steel rod passes loosely. To the ends of the second cross piece, a pair of steel rods are fixed, which are secured at the upper ends to a cross bar connected with the pendulum spring. The expansion of the steel rods would cause the bob to be lowered, whilst the expansion of the zinc rods would raise the bob, the whole being so designed that these two effects neutralize one another. In Harrison's original arrangement, nine rods, five of steel and four of brass, were used instead of five in the simpler modification shown.

This reduction in the number of rods is rendered possible owing to zinc expanding to a greater extent than brass, with the same rise of temperature. For this reason, zinc has for a long time been used instead of brass in pendulums of this type.

Owing to its small coefficient of expansion, deal wood is a suitable material for a pendulum rod; and if used with a fairly long zinc cylinder as a bob, a pendulum sufficiently compensated for ordinary purposes can be obtained. The length of the wood is, however, liable to vary with changes of the dampness of the atmosphere; and dry, well-seasoned wood must be used, which should be varnished.

In later modifications of Harrison's pendulum, a series of concentric tubes of steel and zinc are used in place of the series of parallel rods.

It should not be overlooked that the problem of the design of a compensation pendulum is not to keep the centre of gravity of the pendulum in a constant position, but to maintain constancy in the position of the centre of oscillation, which is a more complicated matter, and involves considerations of the distribution of weight at different distances from the point of support.

Dr. C. E. Guillaume, of the Sèvres Bureau of Weights and Measures, has carried out a series of investigations relating to the properties of alloys of nickel and steel, in the first place for the purpose of obtaining a material suitable for use as a standard of length. He discovered that a mixture can be made, consisting of about 36 per cent of nickel and 64 per cent of steel, which expands or contracts very slightly indeed with changes of temperature. Its coefficient of expansion is about one-twelfth that of ordinary steel, and the introduction of this material for the rods of clock pendulums has rendered the older methods of temperature compensation to a large extent obsolete. It is known as Invar, that is, the first two syllables of the word "invariable," and it is used in the manufacture of modern pendulums for clocks. The necessary compensation for the slight expansion of the invar rod is obtained by adjusting the point of support of the pendulum bob. In one arrangement, a lead bob is attached to the rod at a point below the middle of the bob; and the expansion of the portion of the bob above the point of support tends to cause the clock to gain, while the expansion of the portion below tends to make it lose. The point of support is so adjusted that differences between these two tendencies is a gaining one equal to the loss which would be effected by the slight expansion of the invar rod.

In another arrangement, the bob is supported near its middle point by a tube passing loosely around the pendulum rod and situated in a hole in the lower half of the bob. The tube rests upon nuts at the end of the pendulum rod, and it is made of steel and brass, the respective lengths of the two metals being so chosen that the expansion of this short tube upwards is equal to the total expansion of the long invar rod downwards. In this case, the expansion of the bob itself produces no effect.

The temperature compensation of watches is more difficult than that of pendulum clocks. A rise of temperature increases the dimensions of the balance and causes the watch to lose, and this effect would be magnified by the action of the heat in increasing the length of the balance spring. As, however, the breadth and thickness of the spring are increased at the same time, and an increase in either of these dimensions causes the watch to gain, the total effect of heat on the size only of the spring would mean a gain in the timekeeping, especially as the change in thickness is by far more important than the changes in either length or breadth. Roughly, it may be taken that the loss due to increase in the size of the balance, and the gaining due to increase in the dimensions of the spring, neutralize one another. The greatest factor to be considered, however, is the loss of elasticity of the spring with increasing temperature, which causes the watch to lose, the loss from this cause being much greater than that produced by the increase in size of the balance. A watch with an uncompensated balance would lose about twenty times as much as a clock with an uncompensated steel pendulum; and the problem with which the watchmaker has to deal is comparable with that which would be presented to the clockmaker if the attraction of gravity, instead of being constant, varied with temperature.

In compensating the balances of watches, the principle employed depends upon the different expansions of two metals. If a compound straight bar, consisting of two thin strips of brass and steel fastened together, be heated, the brass will expand more than the steel, and this will cause the bar to bend into a curved shape, the steel being on the inner side of the curve.

About 1760, Harrison applied this principle by mounting the regulator curb pins on one end of a bimetallic strip, which was fixed at the other end; and the bending of the strip, brought about by changes of temperature, altered the position of the pins. This is equivalent to automatically moving the regulator of an ordinary watch whenever any change of temperature occurs, the motion being arranged to take place in the necessary direction and to be of such an amount as to counteract the action of the temperature variation.

As, however, two pairs of curb pins cannot be used on the same spring, this arrangement did not also permit of the ordinary method of regulation. In modifications of this device, a bent bimetallic strip was used, and the change of shape with varying thermal conditions was made to increase or to diminish the distance between the curb pins. Closing the pins causes a watch to gain, while opening them out has a contrary effect. This bent strip was mounted on an ordinary regulating arm, the position of which could be altered as required when the watch went too fast or too slow.

It was explained on page 49 that it was not a satisfactory method of regulating a better class watch by interfering with the length of the balance spring after the most favourable length had been selected to give equal periods of time for long and short arcs of vibration ; and, for the same reason, a temperature compensating device which interferes with the balance spring is not desirable. At an early date, it was recognized that the compensation should be effected by means of the balance and not the spring ; and, about 1765, Pierre Le Roy appears to have first made a balance wheel including a compensating device.

In 1775, Arnold patented a somewhat complicated balance wheel, in which compensation was obtained by means of a bimetallic strip, and shortly afterwards he introduced a simpler arrangement embodying the same principle. Outside and additional to an ordinary balance, he placed two curved arms concentric with the balance, and each projecting an angle of about 120° at the centre. The arms were composite, being of brass outside and of steel inside. When subjected to heat, the arms bent inwards ; and, as they carried adjustable weights on their extremities, it could be so arranged that the gaining effect of the weights being brought nearer the centre, compensated for the loss of time which would otherwise have been caused by the heat.

In a later modification, such as is now used, the bimetallic arms formed the rim of the balance wheel itself, which was not continuous, but was cut at two places near the diametral arm on which the balance was mounted. In the early balances of this type, the two metals were either riveted or soldered together;

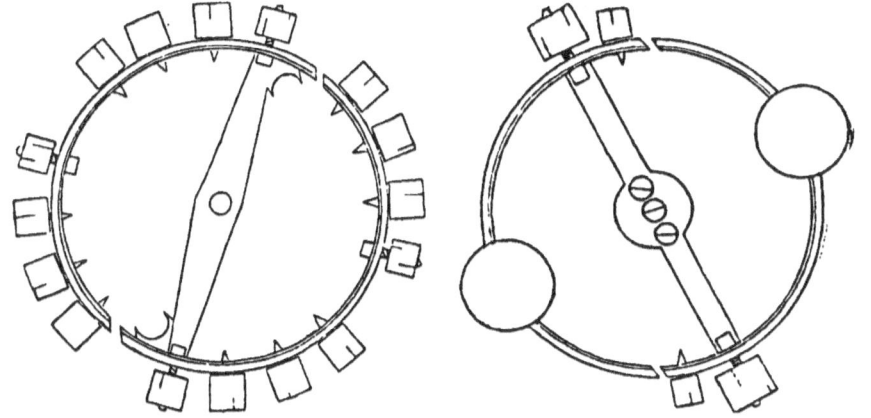

Fig. 16

but, later, a steel disc was immersed in molten brass, some of which attached itself to the rim of the disc, and the balance wheel was constructed from the disc. The credit for this improvement is generally assigned to Earnshaw, but it has been claimed for Brockbank, by whom Earnshaw was at one time employed. The bimetallic rims carry weights, the positions of which can be varied to give the necessary adjustments. Fig. 16 shows two types of compensation balances, one as used in pocket watches and the other as used in ships' chronometers. In the former, there are four screws at right angles for the purpose of regulating the watch as described on page 49 ; and as there are about twenty-four or more holes in the rim, the positions of the other screws shown can be varied to give the necessary compensations for temperature, or they may be exchanged for heavier or lighter screws if required. The balance for a ship's chronometer is fitted with two circular weights, the position of which are adjusted to give the necessary compensations, the effect being greater the nearer the weights are to the free ends of the half rims on which they are mounted. Two timing screws, at the ends of the diametral arm, are employed ; and, in addition, two small supplementary timing screws are shown, which are also of use in poising the balance wheel.

Other conditions being constant, the time of vibration of a balance varies as the square root of the moment of inertia, and inversely as the square root of the modulus of elasticity of the material of the spring. The moment of inertia is obtained by taking the mass of each particle of the balance and multiplying it by the square of its distance from the centre, and then adding together the quantities so obtained for all the particles of the balance. Thus, if any particle were moved to twice the distance from the centre, its contribution towards the total moment of inertia would be increased four times. From this it follows that when the bimetallic rim of a compensation balance bends inwards a certain amount, it effects a change in the moment of inertia, which is smaller than the corresponding change when it bends outward to the same extent.

Approximately, we may take it that the rim bends inward or outward through amounts proportional to the change of temperature, and that the change in the elasticity is roughly (though not exactly) proportional to the variation of temperature. Consequently, if the balance is so adjusted that for a certain rise of temperature the rim with its weight bends inward sufficiently to reduce the moment of inertia by the amount necessary to compensate for the change in the spring, for an equal fall of temperature it will bend out the same amount and overcompensate for the change in the spring. For this reason, an ordinary compensation balance can be adjusted accurately for two extreme temperatures only, and at intermediate temperatures there is an error which is known as the "middle temperature error." Various auxiliary compensating devices have been invented to overcome this error in chronometers; and one patented by E. T. Loseby in 1852, which has features in common with Le Roy's original balance, illustrates the principle employed. At the ends of the bimetallic arms of the balance he mounted small bulbs, which contained mercury and communicated with curved tubes into which the mercury expanded with rise of temperature, as in a thermometer. The curved tubes were so shaped that, as the temperature increased, the direction in which the end of the mercury column moved, more nearly approached that of a radius of the balance. For an increase of temperature, the mercury consequently moved more directly towards the centre of the balance than it receded for an equivalent fall from the same initial temperature.

Chronometers for the Royal Navy are supplied with auxiliary or secondary compensating devices, and an accuracy of 1 in 500,000 can thus be attained.

Reference has already been made to the alloy of nickel and steel, known as invar, which makes it possible practically to dispense with temperature compensation devices in pendulums; but by varying the percentages of nickel, and sometimes adding other metals, different results can be obtained. Dr. Guillame has succeeded in obtaining a nickel-steel alloy, the coefficient of expansion of which varies with the temperature in such a manner that, when this alloy is used together with brass to form a compensation balance, the middle temperature error is eliminated and compensation is obtained at all temperatures. M. Ditisheim, a well-known Swiss maker, with watches employing this new balance, recently obtained record certificates in the Kew and the National Physical Laboratory trials. His watch, which was placed first in the 1920 trials, was a keyless going-barrel two-day watch with a double roller. Its mean change of daily rate for 1° F. change of temperature was ·009 sec.; but other watches, with Guillame balances lower on the list, gave even better performances in this respect.

In his Guthrie lecture to the Physical Society of London in 1920, Dr. Guillame dealt with " The Anomaly of the Nickel-Steels," and it appears that it is not unlikely that this new balance-wheel will soon be displaced by the employment of a balance spring made of an alloy which has the same elasticity at all ordinary temperatures, and that the need for any compensation will cease to exist.

Nickel-steel is also used for the balance springs of ordinary watches and, according to Dr. Guillame, 3,000,000 watches are fitted with such springs every year. Balances consisting of one metal only are used, and the error is about one-twelfth to one-fifteenth of that obtained when an ordinary steel spring is employed.

CHAPTER VIII

THE CHRONOMETER
AND FAMOUS ENGLISH HOROLOGISTS

ONE of the most valuable uses of accurate timekeeping is in connection with navigation. From astronomical observations, the local mean time at any place can be determined, and the difference between this time and Greenwich mean time depends upon the longitude of the place. Consequently, if a vessel starts on her voyage with a chronometer which indicates Greenwich mean time and continues to go accurately throughout the voyage, it is possible on any day to find the longitude of the ship's position if astronomical observations can be made to determine the local mean time. In actual practice, it is not possible to arrange for the ship's chronometer to show always exact Greenwich time, as the best timekeepers have a slight losing or gaining rate. If, however, this rate be known and keeps constant, a simple calculation will enable the exact Greenwich mean time to be determined when required, if the error at the commencement of the voyage is known.

The importance of an accurate timekeeper on board ships for this purpose has long been recognized.

In the early part of the sixteenth century, a Dutch astronomer, Gemma Frisius, proposed the use of portable clocks on board ships; and about 1660-65, pendulum-controlled timepieces were tried, and were found unsatisfactory owing to the motion of the vessel. Another objection to the use of pendulum timekeepers for this purpose is that the time of vibration of a pendulum even if its length remains constant, varies with the latitude of the place. At the equator, the attraction of gravity is less than at the poles, with the result that the time of a vibration of the same pendulum at the equator would be greater than at the poles.

Rewards were offered by various Governments to inventors who succeeded in solving the problem of determining the longitude at sea; and in 1598, the King of Spain offered 100,000 crowns. In Beckmann's *History of Inventions*, it is stated that " what was the opinion then entertained of the nature of the task to be accomplished by means of the balance watches then in use, may be gathered from an expression of Morin, who wrote about the year 1630, and who, in speaking to the Cardinal Richelieu of the difficulty of constructing an instrument which should keep time to the requisite degree of accuracy for that purpose, is reported to have said : ' I know not what such an undertaking would be even to the devil himself, but to man it would undoubtedly be the height of folly.' "

The British Government, in 1714, offered a reward of £10,000 to anyone who invented a method of determining the longitude within an accuracy of 1° during a voyage to the West Indies and back ; while for closer accuracies within 40' and 30', the reward was to be £15,000 and £20,000 respectively. The last-mentioned sum was awarded in instalments to John Harrison, the final residue being paid about 1773.

John Harrison was born in Yorkshire in 1693, and when he was 7 years old his father migrated to Barrow, in Lincolnshire. He was brought up to his father's trade of carpenter and joiner, but he was very much interested in matters relating to clocks. In spite of his early restrictions, John Harrison introduced several important improvements, and from about 1726 onwards he persevered in attempts to fulfil the necessary conditions for the award in connection with the determination of longitude.

His first attempt was with a chronometer, which, in 1736, was tried on a voyage to Lisbon, and the results were sufficiently satisfactory to justify the Board of Longitude in awarding him a gratuity of £500. Subsequently he made other timepieces, and his fourth example was tried in 1761-4. In the former year, his son William took charge of the chronometer on a voyage to Jamaica on board H.M.S. *Deptford*, and also during the return voyage on the *Merlin* in 1762. After eighteen days on the outward journey, there was a difference of about a degree and a half between the longitude as determined by the chronometer and as estimated by the captain, and grave doubts arose as to the reliability of the timepiece. Harrison's son, however, persuaded the captain to trust to the chronometer determination, and his confidence proved to be justified.

The observations indicated an accuracy within the limit of 30′, and a further reward was granted. Certain objections, however, were made and a second trial on a voyage to the Barbadoes took place in 1764. During the voyage out, it is said that the chronometer was of service to the ship's master; and at the end of the return journey it was found that the total error over a period of 156 days, after correcting for the previously declared rate of one second gain in twenty-four hours, was a gain of 54 secs. This was equivalent to an error of 13·5′ longitude, and the performance was considered satisfactory. After it had been ascertained that a description was available from which other makers could construct a similar chronometer, the full award was granted. About the same time, in 1774, regulations were formulated relating to future awards. A duplicate was made by Mr. Larcum Kendal, and was used at sea by Captain Cook. Both it and Harrison's originals are now in the custody of the Astronomer-Royal ; and descriptions of Harrison's first and fourth timepieces were included in a paper on " The History of the Chronometer," read by Lieut.-Com. R. T. Gould, R.N., before the Royal Geographical Society in December, 1920.

The relations between Harrison and the Board of Longitude, upon whom rested the responsibility for certifying that the reward was due, were not altogether friendly, and a full account of the negotiations with reference to the various instalments of the award would be much more complicated than the brief summary just given indicates.

In spite of its great historical importance, Harrison's chronometer was too complicated to be regarded as a practical success capable of general use on ships. The cost of construction was estimated by Kendal at about £400, and the temperature compensation was by means of the curb compensator, which is not so good as the compensation balance. It included, however, his going fusee for maintaining a driving force on the wheel train when the appliance was being wound up, and this feature still survives in modern fusee watches.

Another early maker of chronometers was Thomas Mudge. He was born in 1717, and was the son of a schoolmaster. At the age of 14, he was apprenticed as a watchmaker to George Graham, to whose business he succeeded ; but in 1771 he retired from London and devoted his energies to the solution of the longitude problem. Unfortunately for himself, he did not enter for the longitude trials until after 1774, when the maximum prize offered was £10,000 and more stringent conditions were imposed. His first chronometer was made in 1774, and was tried by the Astronomer-Royal in 1776 and onwards. In 109 days it gained only 1 min. 19 secs., and Mudge was awarded £500 to enable him to supply two more chronometers, which he thought he could make more perfect than his first. This, however, had been found to be superior to any previously tried. He then made two timekeepers, which, for descriptive purposes, were designated " blue " and " green," blue being now exhibited in the Science Museum, South Kensington.

A series of trials continued until 1790, when the Astronomer-Royal reported to the Board of Longitude that not one of the three chronometers had satisfied the required conditions. As in the case of Harrison, there was an acrimonious discussion between the inventor and the Board of Longitude ; and the Astronomer-Royal (Dr. Nevil Maskelyne) was charged with being prejudiced against the possibility of accurately determining the longitude by means of chronometers and with favouring the alternative lunar method, in which the angular distance of the moon from the sun or certain fixed stars is used with reference to tables to determine the Greenwich mean time.

Mudge had the advantage of a barrister son to assist him in his protests ; and, following upon the report of a Select Committee of the House of Commons in 1793, he was awarded an additional £2,500.

In fairness to Dr. Maskelyne, it should be mentioned that, although Admiral Campbell and other navigators commended Mudge's chronometer after experience at sea with it, trials at sea alone were not sufficient. Accurate determinations of the errors from day to day could only be made on land.

Mudge died in 1794, and his son, also Thomas Mudge, established a workshop in which a limited number of chronometers of his father's design were made. They were sold at a price of 150 guineas each, and even at this high price there was a loss.

Like Harrison's chronometer, Mudge's was too complicated and too expensive to be generally introduced for use on ships, and both were soon rendered obsolete by the simpler and more accurate chronometers of Arnold and Earnshaw.

John Arnold was born in 1736 at Bodmin, and was the son of a watchmaker. He commenced work in his father's shop, but afterwards left home for Holland. There he is said to have learnt watchmaking, and he subsequently returned to England. After a period of adversity, he started business near the Strand, and came under the notice of King George III. To that monarch, in 1764, he presented a very small repeating watch of his own manufacture. The diameter of the movement was about that of a silver twopenny piece, and it was set in a ring. It had a cylinder escapement, which is said to have included the first ruby cylinder ever made. This gift so pleased the King, that he presented Arnold with 500 guineas. A foreign monarch offered Arnold 1,000 guineas for a similar watch; but this offer was declined, as Arnold desired the King's repeater to remain unique.

His chronometer does not appear to have been formally entered for the longitude trials, but examples of it were under observation by the Astronomer-Royal at Greenwich Observatory at the same time as Mudge's, and it was reported that Arnold's was the better. During his life he received grants from the Board of Longitude amounting to £1,322; and after his death, which occurred in 1799, it was decided to make a total award of £3,000, the balance of £1,678 being paid to his son.

Arnold's chronometer represented a considerable advance over its predecessors. The temperature compensation was confined to the balance without any interference with the balance spring; and the latter was made in the form of a cylindrical spiral, which still survives in modern ships' chronometers. It is said that Arnold's timepiece was the first to which the word "chronometer" was applied, although that word had previously been used in connection with metronomes. Many examples were made and, in addition to its use on ships, the chronometer was adapted for pocket watches. Arnold's escapement is, however, not now employed, as an escapement due to Earnshaw was found to be better.

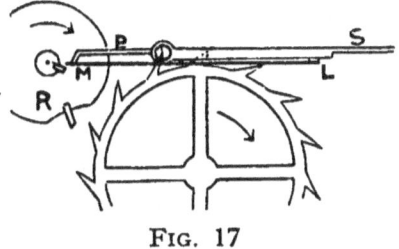

FIG. 17

Thomas Earnshaw was born at Ashton-under-Lyne, Lancashire, in 1749; and when 14 years old was apprenticed to the watch trade. Subsequently he came to London and for many years had a business at 119 High Holborn. He made important contributions towards the progress of horology, and the chronometer escapement still in use is of the form introduced by him about 1782. This escapement is illustrated in Fig. 17. The escape wheel has 15 teeth, and is prevented from moving by one of the teeth resting against a jewel locking stone. This stone is mounted upon a bar including a strip spring S, and from the free end of the bar, or detent, a bent arm P projects in the direction of the balance wheel. Mounted on the detent is a fine strip spring of gold, LM, with which a jewelled unlocking pallet, mounted near the axis of the balance wheel, engages. When the balance vibrates in the direction indicated by the arrow, the unlocking pallet merely pushes the fine spring aside and encounters little resistance, as the spring is then caused to bend along its whole length; on the return swing, however, the spring is pushed against the arm P projecting from the detent and, as only a very short portion of the spring overlaps the arm, this short length is stiff enough to cause the detent to be moved by the motion of the unlocking pallet. The detent moves sufficiently to release the tooth of the escape wheel and the latter moves forward, one of its teeth engaging with a jewelled impulse pallet mounted on the disc R, which is attached to the balance wheel's axis. An impulse is then given to the balance, and the next tooth of the escape wheel is locked by the jewel of the detent.

During the first swing of the balance, it was free except for the practically negligible bending of the thin gold spring; while, on the return swing, there was the bending of the detent spring, instantly followed by the impulse received from the escape wheel. The impulse pallet upon which the escape wheel acts is moving at its maximum rate when it receives an impulse, and the wheel is not checked in its motion in the same manner as is the escape wheel of a lever watch when its teeth engage with the pallets. As a result, when watching a chronometer escapement in action, one cannot notice the actual movement of the wheel teeth. There appears to be an indistinct trembling, however, and it is necessary to look at the arms of the wheel to confirm that the latter is rotating.

Arnold's escapement was similar in principle to Earnshaw's; but the detent was bent towards the centre of the escape wheel when the impulse was to be given, and the ends of the teeth projected upward to make this arrangement possible. The faces of the teeth which gave the impulse were curved, instead of being straight as in Earnshaw's escapement. Earlier detent escapements had been made by the French horologist Pierre Le Roy, who, however, mounted the detent on pivots instead of on the end of a spring. Le Roy's chronometer escapement of 1748 was the first detached escapement, and among the many interesting exhibits in the Conservatoire des Arts et Métiers, Paris, there is a famous chronometer made by him in 1766.

Earnshaw's chronometers were tried for the Board of Longitude, but their performances were judged not to have come within the prescribed limits. Dr. Maskelyne was, however, favourably impressed by them, and considered that they would be of great use in navigation, and Earnshaw received a total award of £3,000, which was equal to the awards allotted to Mudge and to Arnold.

In addition to Harrison, Mudge, Arnold, and Earnshaw, there were famous horologists who were not directly associated with the chronometer and the determination of longitude trials, but who, nevertheless, during the seventeenth and eighteenth centuries did much towards establishing the recognized pre-eminence of English watches, which were much appreciated by the wealthy of all countries.

Prominent among these horologists is Thomas Tompion, who was born in 1639, and is often spoken of as "the father of English watchmaking." It is said that he was originally a farrier, and that his experience of clocks commenced with a meat-jack. He made many famous clocks and watches, but it was falsely published about 1700 that he was making a clock for St. Paul's Cathedral which would go 100 years without being wound up. The balance spring was introduced by Hooke, who appears to have been assisted by Tompion in overcoming the practical difficulties of the application. The latter also assisted Barlow in a similar manner with reference to the rack-striking mechanism. One of the first watches to be constructed with a balance spring was made for Charles II, and was inscribed : " Robt. Hooke, invenit 1658. Thos. Tompion, fecit 1675."

Tompion died in 1713, and bequeathed his business to George Graham, who had been associated with him from the time when the latter completed his apprenticeship. Graham was born in Cumberland in 1673, and he became one of the greatest horologists of his day, in addition to establishing a reputation as an inventor and an improver of astronomical instruments. His inventions include the mercurial compensation pendulum and the dead-beat escapement for clocks, and also the cylinder escapements for watches, which devices have already been described. He was a Fellow of the Royal Society, a member of the Society of Friends, and was highly esteemed for his work and for his personal character. In November, 1751, he died in his seventy-eighth year, and was buried in Westminster Abbey in the same grave as Tompion.

CHAPTER IX

CLOCK AND WATCH CASES

THE decorative features of clocks and watches, with their interesting examples of craftsmanship in metal and wood work, appeal to many people who are not much concerned with the mechanical and scientific principles of horology. Many collectors show great enthusiasm for old clock cases; and it is not at all unusual to find modern movements in old cases, the original movements having been discarded without any regrets.

The earliest clocks, being of large size for public use, were not encased, and may be taken as examples mainly of engineers' and smiths' work, although the dials and the accessory figures, used for striking the bells and representing supplementary complications, often included decorative features of great interest.

Table clocks were introduced in Germany in the early part of the sixteenth century, and followed the invention of the driving spring. They consisted of spring-driven movements, with verge escapements controlled by balances which were not provided with balance springs. Owing to their being spring-driven, they were portable and were not subject to the restrictions as to their positions which apply to weight-driven clocks. Some of these table clocks were enclosed in square boxes, with sides of iron decorated with gold scrolls. On the top there was a dial indicating the hours, and on the bottom there were sometimes dials connected with astronomical phenomena.

Other table clocks of this period were placed in round

cases, which were occasionally supplied with perforated domes.

These clocks were too expensive for general use, and the English domestic clock for ordinary houses may be considered to have originated with the lantern or birdcage clock, which was introduced about the end of the sixteenth century. The movement was placed in a brass case surmounted by a bell, but the driving weights and the cords supporting them were outside the case. In the early examples, there was, of course, no pendulum, and a verge escapement was employed ; but the foliot bar balance used in the earliest clocks was replaced by a wheel. After about 1660, when the pendulum was introduced, it was applied to these clocks, a short pendulum being employed, which was sometimes placed in front of the dial, though more often it was behind. Clocks of this type were secured to a wall or mounted on a bracket, and the weights were wound up by pulling at the opposite end of the cord to that to which the weight was attached. Towards the end of the seventeenth century, the long or royal pendulum was applied, and the greater part of the pendulum then came outside the case.

Generally, there was only one hand, which indicated the hours ; and the train of wheels for the going and striking portions were not placed side by side between the same plates, as in modern clocks. The striking train was mounted separately at the back. Some forms of lantern clocks had large dials, which overlapped the sides of the movement in a marked manner, and these were known as sheep's-head clocks.

In the latter part of the seventeenth century, clocks were made in which only the movement was enclosed by a wooden case. These are known as " hood " clocks, and constitute the intermediate stage between the brass-cased lantern clock and the later " grandfather " clock. The weights were external, as in the lantern clock, and the case was mounted on a wall. Supporting the movement, there were generally two brackets secured to the back board, while above the dial there was an extension upward of the hood. Dutch clocks of this type, such as the Friesland and the Zaandam clocks, were very elaborately decorated, and the bob of the pendulum often took the form of an animal or other figure.

The long-cased " grandfather " clock appears to have been introduced just before or about the same time as the invention of the anchor escapement in 1675. The cheaper cases were made of oak; but the better examples included marquetry, in which veneers on thin strips of high grade woods of different colours were combined to form an inlaid pattern representing floral or other designs.

Marquetry work continued to be used for clock cases from about 1675 to about 1715, when it appears to have gone out of fashion, although it was revived to a limited extent towards the end of the eighteenth century under the influence of Sheraton and others.

Lacquered decorations in green, red, black, and gold colours were employed on long-cased clocks during the first three quarters of the eighteenth century. The designs were generally Oriental in style; and clock cases, made in England, were sometimes sent in tea ships to China or Japan to be lacquered. This system of decoration was especially popular about the middle of the century. In a typical example, the hinged door and the base are lacquered in green and gold, the design including a building, flowers, and a group of figures, one of which is mounted on horseback.

In the latter half of the eighteenth century, mahogany came into use as the favourite material for veneering long clock cases, and its use is sometimes associated with the influence of Thomas Chippendale.

Bracket clocks may be regarded as a development of the early table clocks, which have previously been mentioned. They are spring-driven and have short cases. Their use continued throughout the period of the long-cased clock. The late seventeenth-century examples have verge escapements, with short pendulums, and are generally enclosed in black wood cases. At the top there is a handle for carrying the clock, and immediately below there is frequently a gilt basket-work decoration. The back plate is engraved with ornamental designs, which are rendered visible by a glass door at the back. Although lantern clocks were usually mounted on brackets, they are not described as bracket clocks, that term being somewhat strangely confined to a type of clock which can be easily removed from one position to another.

The earliest watches were small table clocks in cylindrical cases, generally with a hinged front cover. Gilt brass was a common material for the construction of the case, but the movement itself was of steel. There was no glass at the front, and the front cover was perforated to enable the position of the hand to be seen. These watches, and those which immediately succeeded them, were not designed for being carried in a pocket. If small enough to be attached to the person, they were carried by a chain passing round the neck. The cases of sixteenth and early seventeenth century watches of this type took various forms. Some people appear to have had a preference for a skull-shaped case, in which a portion of the skull, such as the lower jaw, was hinged to serve as a front cover of the case and enable the dial in the interior to be inspected. Cruciform and octagonal cases were also used, in addition to representations of flowers, animals, books, and butterflies. In the early part of the seventeenth century, flat oval, or egg-shaped cases were popular, and watches so cased were named "Nuremberg eggs."

The fob, or small pocket for carrying a watch, appears to have been introduced about 1625, and it has been suggested that it was due to the influence of the Puritans. About the same time, a circular-shaped case, suitable for the pocket, became popular. Originally, single cases were used; but in the middle of the seventeenth century, an outer case was added, resulting in the pair cases which continued to be made until the early part of the nineteenth century.

Various methods have been employed for the decoration of watch cases, and there are many interesting examples of enamelled work. One of the examples in the Victoria and Albert Museum was made by Goullons, of Paris, about 1640, and has an enamelled gold case. On the outside there are representations of the Holy Family and the Virgin and Child; while inside the case are portraits of Louis XIII and Cardinal Richelieu. The case is about $2\frac{1}{2}$ ins. diameter, and the enamel is attributed to Henri Toutin.

Repoussé work was used to a considerable extent during the seventeenth and eighteenth centuries for the purpose of ornamenting cases. In this work, the metal is embossed by hammering or pressing from behind the surface to be decorated; and the design generally, though not always, projected prominently from the surface. This form of decoration was mainly applied to the outer cases of watches with pair cases, and the inner cases sometimes had pierced decorations.

Tortoiseshell, leather, fish skin, and shagreen are some of the materials which have been employed for the outer surfaces of pair cases. An alloy of zinc and copper, known as "pinchbeck," was extensively used for watch cases during the eighteenth century. It had the appearance of gold, and was named after its inventor, Christopher Pinchbeck, who was also a famous horologist.

During the latter part of the eighteenth century and the greater part of the nineteenth century, a form of decoration, known as engine-turning, was among the various forms in use. Wavy lines were cut on the case by means of a lathe, in which the work was mounted. The mandrel was not fixed, but was urged by a spring against a rotating cam, which was circular in general outline, but the circumference was indented so that it took the shape of a wavy line. As the cam rotated, it imparted a chattering motion to the mandrel and work, and so caused the fixed cutter to produce on the work a wavy circle similar in shape to the circumference of the cam. A series of such concentric wavy circles were cut to cover the back of a case, and between the successive cuts the work was rotated with reference to the cam, so that the troughs of one set of waves rested on the crests of the next inner set. This produced an effect of curved lines apparently proceeding from the centre to the outer rim of the case, although actually all the lines employed were wavy circles. Although useful in preventing marks due to slight scratches being obvious, this form of decoration is no longer popular.

Numerous illustrations of interesting clock cases are reproduced in Cescinsky and Webster's *English Domestic Clocks* and Britten's *Old Clocks and Watches and their Makers*, the latter also containing representations of watches.

CHAPTER X

ELECTRIC CLOCKS

THE applications of electricity to horology take several forms. Electricity may be used merely to dispense with the necessity of winding a clock by hand, and the electrically-driven clocks so obtained are of two types. In one type, the clock closely resembles the ordinary form, and is driven by a spring or a weighted arm, which is wound up at a regular interval of, say, 10 mins. or an hour, by the action of an electric current ; while in the other type, the pendulum itself is maintained in vibration by electrical means, and is used to propel the train of wheel indicating the time.

When properly constructed, an electrically-driven clock continues going for a long time ; but if it does not include any device for correcting its errors, these will accumulate and, as far as the clock's use as an indicator of time is concerned, it would often be desirable for such a clock to stop. Most clocks need attention at intervals for the correction of the time and the regulation of the rate, and when a clock is wound by hand such needs are usually noticed. There does not appear to be any considerable advantage in an electrical application which merely drives the clock, although the inventions for that purpose include some very interesting devices.

Of greater utility are the synchronized systems, in which a number of clocks, which may be of the ordinary spring or weight-driven type; are connected with a central standard or master clock, with which they are made to agree. This has been achieved in some systems by causing all the pendulums to vibrate in unison, while in other systems an ordinary clock has its hands forcibly corrected every hour.

In another system of electric clocks, which has been extensively developed in recent years, the master clock is connected with a number of impulse dial mechanisms, in which the ordinary driving portion of a clock is absent. Every half-minute the master clock transmits electric currents to the dials, which cause their hands to jump forward through the space of half a minute. Such dials can clearly not be used to indicate the time to a small fraction of a minute, but they give a reading which is sufficiently accurate for ordinary purposes; while their connection with the master clock, which is kept accurately to time, prevents accumulation of errors.

The earliest electric clock in England to attain any practical success was probably that invented by Alexander Bain about 1843, in which electricity was employed to propel the pendulum. Its action depends upon the fact that while an electric current passes through a coil of wire, the coil behaves as a magnet, one end of it corresponding with the north pole of an ordinary magnet and the other end with a south pole. As the north pole of a magnet is repelled by the north pole of another magnet and attracted by the south pole, it follows that the north pole of the coil will be repelled by another north pole, while the south pole of the coil will be attracted by a north pole. On the end of a pendulum, Bain mounted a coil of wire of many turns; while secured to the case there were two curved magnets with their north poles facing one another, so arranged that the coil could swing while embracing the magnets. The pendulum moved a sliding piece which made the electrical contacts, and at the end of a swing to the left the electrical circuit was closed and a current passed through the coil during the next swing to the right. The coil was then attracted by one of the fixed magnets and repelled by the other, and at the end of the swing the sliding piece had been moved again by the pendulum, so that the circuit was broken and a current no longer passed through the coil. Under the action of gravity, the pendulum then swung to the left and again closed the circuit at the end of its swing. The pendulum was thus maintained in vibration by impulses given to it every alternate swing. If, however, the arc of vibration exceeded a certain amount, the pendulum carried the sliding piece beyond the stud by which the electrical contact was made, and no impulse was given during the next swing.

Near its upper end, the pendulum carried a pawl which engaged with a ratchet wheel and propelled the wheel work connected with the hands of the clock.

As a source of electrical energy, Bain employed plates of zinc and copper buried in the earth, and he also arranged for a series of impulse dials in connection with the pendulum.

Electro-magnets have been extensively used in electric clocks : they consist of coils of wire wound round soft iron cores. While a current is passing through such a coil, the core becomes magnetized and forms a much more powerful magnet than the coil itself would be without the core. Being of soft iron, the latter does not retain its magnetism after the current ceases to flow ; and by mounting a piece of soft iron, known as an armature, on the pendulum and providing for this to be attracted by an electro-magnet during the latter portion of the first half of a swing, a pendulum can be kept in vibration. It is so arranged that when the pendulum reaches its lowest position, the electro-magnet ceases to be excited. Hipp's electric clock, introduced about 1842, embodies this principle, but it is so designed that the pendulum receives an impulse only when its arc of vibration falls below a certain amount. In addition to a soft iron armature moving over an electro-magnet, the pendulum carries a short-hinged piece or trailer, which comes into contact with a notched block mounted on a strip spring. When the arc of swing is great enough, the trailer moves clear of the block each vibration; but when the arc falls below a certain amount, the trailer does not clear the block at the end of a swing and, during the next swing, the end of the trailer is pushed into the notch by the returning pendulum, and the block and its spring are depressed to allow the pendulum and trailer to pass. When depressed, the spring makes contact with a second spring below and closes the electrical circuit, with the result that the armature of the pendulum is attracted by the electro-magnet, which, however, ceases to be excited when the pendulum reaches its middle position, as the trailer is of such a length that it does not depress the spring after the middle position is reached. The attraction of the armature increases the velocity of the pendulum and thus imparts an impulse which increases its arc of vibration, and a number of swings follow without any impulse, until the arc of vibration again becomes small enough to produce a repetition of the process described.

C. H. Pond's electric clock, which was introduced in 1881, is of the ordinary spring-driven type, but the spring is wound up once an hour by a small electric motor, which is brought into action by a contact made by the wheel work of the clock. The clocks made by the Self-Winding Clock Company, U.S.A., which are used on the London electric railways, are of the same type, and are automatically wound up every hour, the motor employed having an action similar to the ordinary electric trembler bell. The arm, which ordinarily would carry a hammer to strike the bell, is provided with a pawl engaging with ratchet work connected with the driving spring of the clock.

In 1858, Mr. R. L. Jones introduced a system of synchronization in which a number of connected weight-driven clocks were employed, each of which had a pendulum and fixed magnets of the type used in Bain's clock. A controlling standard clock included a pendulum represented by O in Fig. 18, which made electrical contacts each swing and caused currents successively in opposite directions to be transmitted through the coils, R, of the pendulums of the connected clocks, of which only one is shown in the diagram. If the pendulum of one of these connected clocks tended to lag behind the standard clock, the effect of the current was to urge it forward ; while, conversely, if it were inclined to go faster than the standard clock, the currents retarded its motion. The series of clocks were thus kept in unison with the controller. This system was developed by Messrs. James Ritchie & Son, Edinburgh, who constructed " electro-sympathetic " clocks embodying the same principle, in which, however, the connected pendulums, instead of being merely controlled by the currents from the standard clock, were driven by those currents, the ordinary weight-driving mechanism being eliminated.

In these electro-sympathetic clocks, the hand work was driven by means of a reversed gravity escapement, shown in Fig. 19. The pendulum P in its vibrations successively displaces the gravity arms A and B, and, on their return motions, these arms actuate the escape wheel S, causing it to rotate.

An interesting method whereby an electric standard

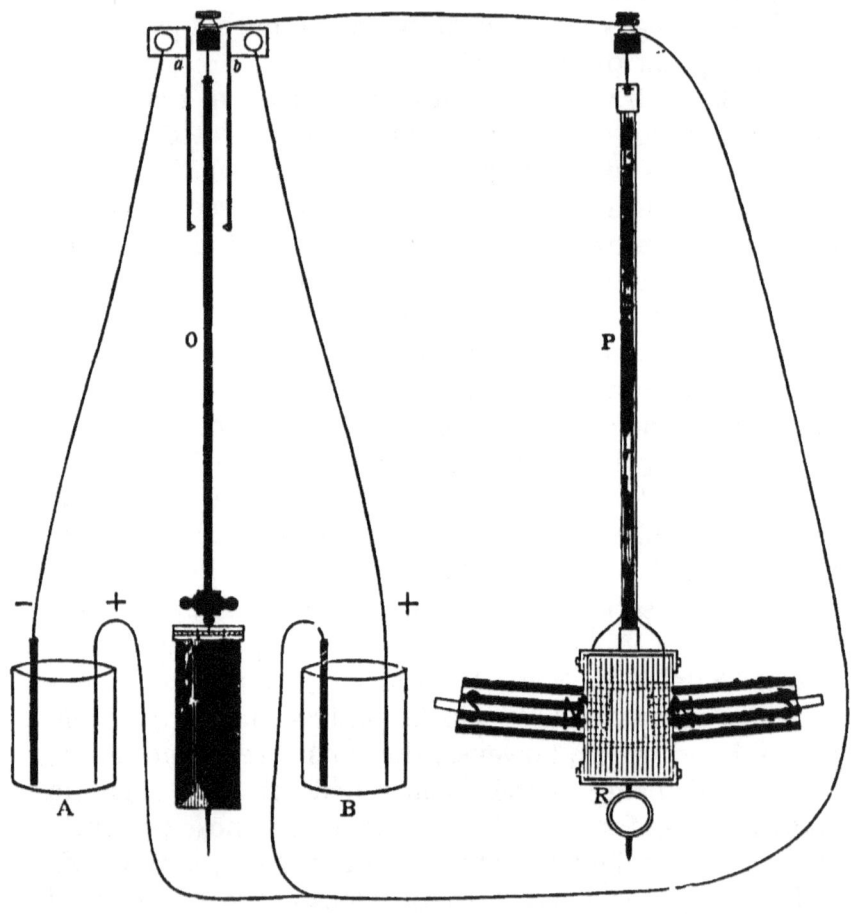

Fig. 18

clock can be employed to control the pendulum of an ordinary clock has been recently introduced by Messrs. Gent & Co., primarily for use in connection with workmen's time registers. The device is known as the " reflex " pendulum control, and is illustrated in Fig. 20. A flat spring is attached to the pendulum of the clock to be controlled, and normally, as the pendulum swings, the tip of the spring just passes clear of the teeth of a rack, which is hinged to a fixed piece. The pendulum is so adjusted that the clock, if left to itself, would lose slightly. Every half-minute an electric current transmitted from the standard clock causes the rack to be raised and makes it engage with the strip spring before the pendulum has completed a vibration to the left. The check to which the pendulum is then subjected temporarily increases its rate, with the result that it catches up the time it has lost and keeps time with the standard clock. The slight losing rate of the pendulum ensures that its spring is always above the rack when the correcting current is transmitted.

Various methods have been suggested and used by Breguet, Bain, and others for the forcible correction of the hands of an ordinary clock, Breguet's being a purely mechanical device. Fig. 21 represents a modification of Bain's method, which was employed by Messrs. James Ritchie & Son about 1876. A V-shaped piece, which normally occupies the dotted position, is connected with the armature of an electro-magnet, which is excited at exactly the end of each hour. This raises the V, and the latter engages with a pin projecting from the minute hand in such a manner that the hand is set to the correct time, as shown in the figure.

In an arrangement, patented in 1876 by J. A. Lund, two short arms, situated about the twelve mark of the dial, are made to approach one another in scissors

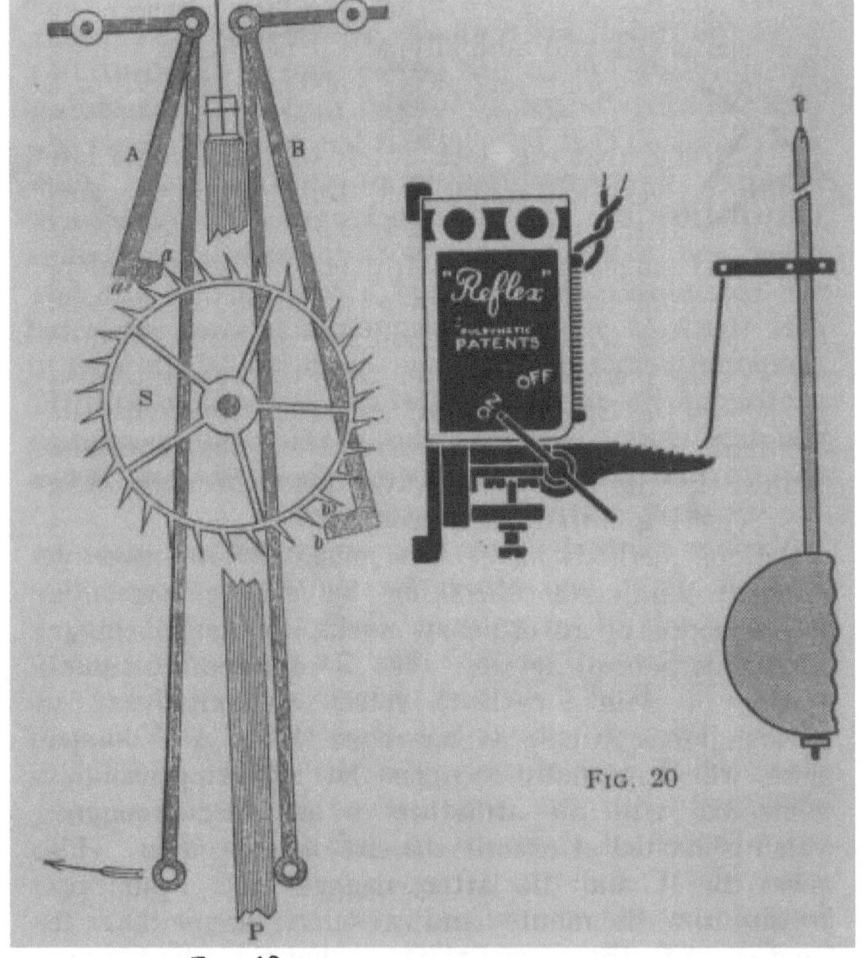

Fig. 19

Fig. 20

fashion, exactly at each hour, by means of controlling currents which excite electromagnets. When closing together, these arms will embrace the end of the minute hand and set it exactly to time. Similar in principle, although differing in detail, is the method adopted on

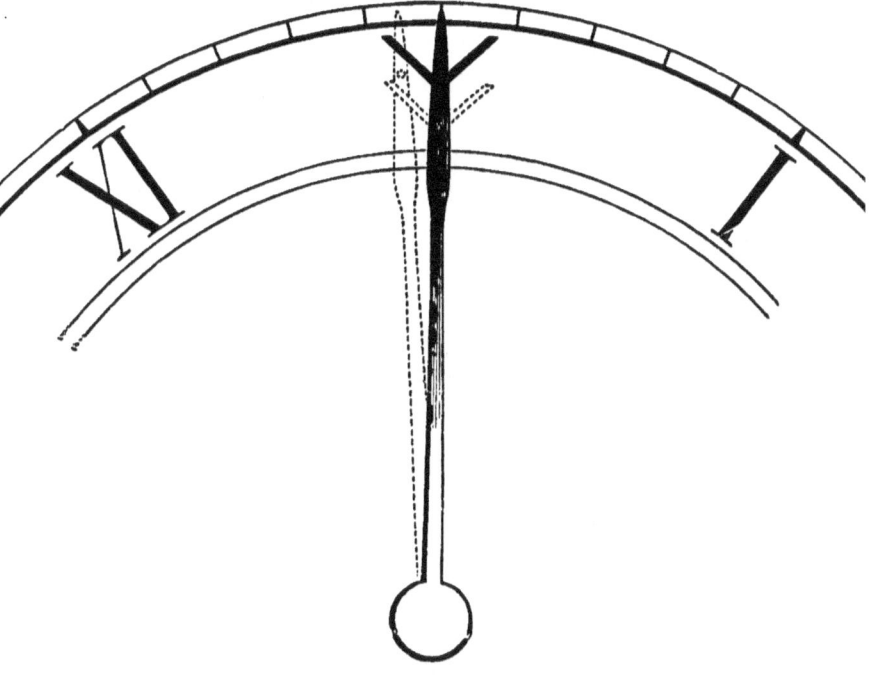

Fig. 21

the clocks used on the London electric railways. A fork-shaped piece, which is depressed by the action of the correcting current, engages with projections on the wheel carrying the minute hand, which is thus corrected hourly. In another method, used by Messrs. Ritchie in 1877, the clock is made to gain slightly, but the minute hand is prevented by a stop from passing the hour position until the stop is rendered ineffective by the action of the correcting current. This principle has been employed by the Post Office authorities.

Probably the most valuable of the applications of electricity to horology are the impulse dial mechanisms, with their connected master clocks or time transmitters. In some of these systems, the pendulum of the master clock receives an impulse every half-minute and, at the same time, it closes the circuit through all the connected dials, the hands of which are advanced through half a minute. These systems are very suitable for the requirements of factories and institutions, for they ensure that the clocks in all the rooms agree with one another in their readings. If the master clock should have gained or lost at all, the arrangements provided for putting it right again are such that all the connected dials are at the same time automatically set to the right time.

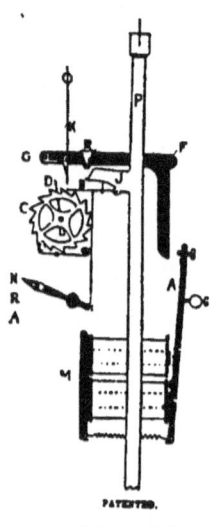

Fig. 22

One of the earliest successful systems of this type is that of the Synchronome Company, with which Mr. F. Hope-Jones is associated; and Fig. 22 shows their master clock. The seconds pendulum, P, carries a light-hinged arm, B, provided at its free end with a jewelled pin or hook, which propels the wheel, C, having 15 teeth and known as the count wheel, by pulling it through the space of one tooth every alternate swing. Mounted diametrically on the wheel, there is a vane, D, which once every revolution engages with a catch, K, and, by pushing it aside, releases the gravity arm, G. When released, this arm falls and a roller on it engages with the inclined face of the pallet piece, J, carried by the pendulum, and imparts an impulse to the pendulum to maintain it in vibration. The tail-piece of the gravity arm engages with the contact on A and completes an electric circuit, which includes all the connected dial mechanisms and also the electro-magnet, M. When energized, the latter

FIG. 23

attracts an armature mounted on the lever, A, which imparts a blow to the tail-piece of the gravity arm and restores it to its normal position, ready for a repetition of the process in half a minute's time.

Fig. 23 shows the Synchronome arrangement of connected dials. B is an electro-magnet, which attracts the armature, C, and when the lever, D, returns under the action of its spring, after the current has ceased to flow, the wheel of 120 teeth is advanced through the space of one tooth, which, as the minute hand is mounted on the wheel, represents half a minute. The stop H and the pin I, which engages with a semi-circular notch in the lever, are for the purpose of preventing more than one tooth being advanced at a time and for locking the wheel.

In the earliest form of dial mechanisms, a simple ratchet and pawl mechanism was employed, with which it was possible for a strong impulse to move the wheel through a space of more than one tooth ; while it was also possible for the hand to be accidentally moved forward. One condition which is now taken as imperative in impulse dials is that the wheel must be locked or positively controlled throughout all the stages of its operation. The first dial to fulfil these conditions was probably that patented by Victor Reclûs in 1886.

Returning to the master clock, if the pointer, which normally is set to N, be moved to R, the arm carrying the hook is raised so that it does not engage with the count wheel ; and during the time that this non-engagement occurs, the count wheel is at rest and no progress is made towards giving an impulse to the dials. In this way, correction can be made for any gaining of time by the clocks. On the other hand, if the clocks are slow, the pointer is set to A, and the hook then engages with the catch of the gravity arm every alternate swing of the pendulum. The arm consequently falls and makes a contact every two seconds, and the dials are moved through half a minute each time until they have been brought to the correct time.

In the " Pulsynetic " system of Messrs. Gent & Co. (*see* Fig. 24), the principle is similar ; but the count wheel is advanced by a push instead of a pull, and one tooth, E_1, of the wheel is more indented than the others. When the driving pawl D, which is mounted on the pendulum H, engages with this deep tooth, its extension D_1 rises and, as the pendulum swings to the right, D_1 pushes aside the stirrup catch S and releases the gravity lever G. This lever carries a

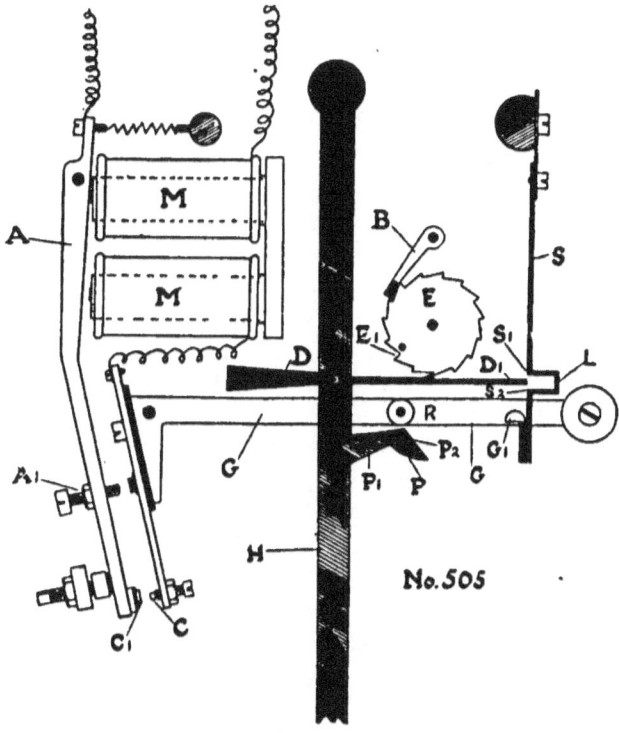

FIG. 24

roller R, which about the middle of the return swing rolls down the inclined face P_2 of the pallet P attached to the pendulum, an impulse towards the left being thus given to the latter. When the deep tooth is not in action, D_1 passes freely into the loop L and the gravity lever is not released. By these means the pendulum receives an impulse once every half-minute, and the gravity lever falls until its contact C meets the contact C_1. An electric circuit is then closed, which operates the connected impulse dials and also energizes the electro-magnet MM. The armature A is then attracted and the gravity lever restored to its normal position. If the batteries of the circuit are getting weak, they become sluggish in action, and a

FIG. 25

longer period elapses before the gravity arm is restored to its normal position. By including an electric bell in the circuit, which is made to ring when the circuit is closed for a long enough period, but does not ring when the batteries are of full strength and the circuit consequently closed for a shorter period only, a warning is obtained when the batteries are failing and requiring attention.

Fig. 25 shows a Pulsynetic impulse dial viewed from

the back, and Fig. 26 represents the Thornbridge transmitter, which is a refined form of Pulsynetic master clock used in some observatories. The movement is jewelled and an impulse is given every two seconds, a seconds hand being provided on the transmitter and its connected impulse clocks.

FIG. 26

Messrs. Gent & Co.'s " waiting train " movement is very interesting, and is designed for turret clocks, where large hands are exposed to the atmosphere and a variable force is required for propelling them in the different conditions of the weather. It consists of two portions, one of which may be regarded as an electric motor for driving the hands. This is shown in Fig. 27, and it consists of a massive electrically-driven pendulum on the Hipp principle, in which an impulse is given to the pendulum whenever its vibrations fall below a certain angle of swing. The pendulum is connected by a pawl, ratchet wheel, and worm-gearing

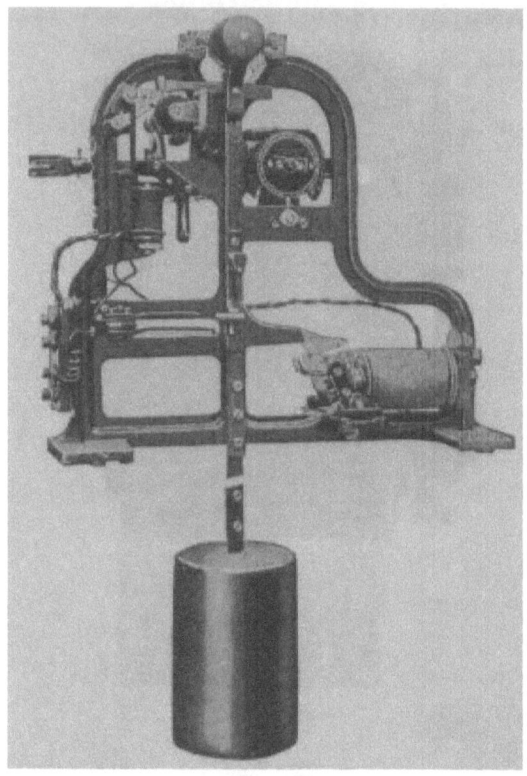

Fig. 27

with the hands, and accurate timekeeping is not one of its functions. It is arranged to move the hands through a space of half a minute in a little under that time, say 27 secs. At the end of that period, the pawl is automatically put out of action, and the movement of the pendulum continues without advancing the hands of the clock. The other portion consists of a Pulsynetic master clock or time transmitter, which keeps accurate time and every half-minute transmits an electric current, which restores the pawl of the pendulum into action again and thus causes the propulsion of the clock hands to be continued through the space of another half-minute. For ordinary purposes, the few seconds' rest of the hands every half-minute is not important. About 1911, a clock of this type, with four dials 25 ft. diameter, was made for the Royal Liver Buildings, Liverpool.

The Silent Electric Company make an impulse dial which consists of a pivoted armature, which is made to rotate by means of electric currents transmitted from a master clock, and communicates its motion to the hand work. The special advantage of this dial is that the use of ratchet wheels and click work, with their attendant noise, is dispensed with, and a quiet action is obtained.

Wireless telegraphy affords a means of distributing time signals over a wide area, and is being increasingly employed for that purpose. From the Eiffel Tower, Paris, and other large stations, signals are sent out at stated times, which may be received with comparatively simple apparatus, and the arrangements are such that no special skill is required on the part of the observer. These signals may also be employed to determine the longitude of a receiving station, and are used for that purpose both by ships at sea and explorers on land.

References often appear to the radium " clock," which is sometimes said to represent the nearest approach to perpetual motion yet achieved.

Radium was discovered in recent years, and it possesses many special properties. It is continually giving out invisible rays of three distinct types. A substance containing a little radium is placed in a highly-exhausted vacuum tube, which also contains two strips of metal foil hanging side by side. The actions of the rays causes these strips to be electrified and to repel one another. They consequently open out and separate until in the extreme position they come in contact with metal pieces at the side of the tube, when they lose their electrical charges and fall into their original positions. This process continues indefinitely with equal intervals of time between the successive discharges ; but there are at present no practical means of automatically indicating the number of times which the strips open and close, and the appliance is not used for indicating the time. Moreover, the period for each operation does not continue to be equal over a number of years. The apparatus is of considerable scientific interest, and is a special form of electroscope. It was devised by the present Lord Rayleigh.

One of the properties of radium is employed to make watch dials and hands visible in the dark, and so enable the time to be read under such conditions. In this case, the alpha rays, which it emits, are used. If these rays fall on zinc sulphide, they render it luminous ; and by using a mixture containing zinc sulphide and a very small quantity of radium to mark the hours and minutes on the dials, these are made visible in darkness. The watch hands are similarly treated.

CHAPTER XI

TRADE

ACCORDING to tradition, the Glastonbury Abbey clock, which was made about 1335, was the work of one man ; and it may be assumed that in the early days of watch- and clock-making, there was no subdivision of labour, such as is now prevalent, and that each workman was qualified to execute the work required in different details of a timekeeper. As, however, clocks and watches came into more general use and were manufactured on a commercial scale, the workman specialized in some branch of clockmaking or watchmaking, and these manufactures were each subdivided into a number of trades. For example, about the middle of the nineteenth century, which was probably its period of greatest magnitude, English watchmaking was divided into about forty branches.

The term "movement" is generally applied to the going part of a watch, apart from the case ; but among the divisions of manufacture, movement-making constituted the construction of the rough movements before they were passed to the watch manufacturer proper to be completed by hand. For the English trade, these rough movements were made mainly at Prescot, in Lancashire ; and they included the plates, pillars, barrel, fusee, wheels with their teeth cut, pinions, and other parts. About 1865, John Wycherly, of Prescot, who was responsible for important improvements in movement-making, introduced a partially finished machine-made movement in which some parts, such as the barrel and fusee arbors, were finished and polished; and the cheaper grades of this movement were sold to the manufacturer at a very low price. At a later date, movements were supplied, in which holes were drilled in the plates, though the wheels had still to be pivoted by hand.

On receiving the movement, the manufacturer passed it in succession to workmen in the various trades. The fusee-cutter made the spiral groove in the fusee; the "first-halver" completed the fusee, the centre, third and fourth wheels, fitted the mainspring, the chain, the detent for the maintaining power, and the stop work to prevent overwinding. The jeweller, motion-maker, dial-maker, dial-painter, case-maker, engraver, gilder, hander, escapement-maker, and finisher were among the trades concerned; while, finally, there was the examiner, upon whom fell the responsibility of checking the accuracy of his predecessors' work.

Formerly English watches were made in considerable numbers in Clerkenwell (London), Coventry, Liverpool, and other places; and the "English lever" was popular not only in this country but abroad. It was a full-plate watch, differing in important respects, especially in the escapement and the addition of a maintaining power, from the English verge of the seventeenth and eighteenth centuries; but it is interesting to note that there had been no revolutionary change in the general arrangement of the movement. To wind the watch up, it was necessary to open the back of the case; to set the hands, the front of the case had to be opened; and for purposes of regulation, it was necessary to swing the whole of the movement out of the case.

Abroad, important improvements were applied. The going-barrel watch was more simple than the fusee type, and was found to be good enough for ordinary purposes, especially where cheapness was a desirable feature. Keyless winding was more difficult to arrange for with the fusee; but, nevertheless, English makers adhered to this device, which is now recognized as an unnecessary refinement for pocket watches. The fusee watch was wound up by rotating the winding-key in the left-hand direction, while the going-barrel watch was wound right-handed. Such was the prejudice in England in favour of the left-handed winding, which was associated sentimentally with the English lever, that some going-barrel watches made in this country were actually arranged for left-handed winding, an additional or idle wheel without any pinion being introduced into the train to permit of this arrangement. With a few exceptions, the English makers failed to respond to the demand for a cheap, reliable watch such as the Swiss and Americans were making by machinery, in which the various parts were made to fixed sizes and subsequently assembled. About 1880 it was probably possible for the English makers to improve the English manufacturing trade, but no adequate general effort was made, and the trade declined. At that time, it may be roughly assumed, the magnitude of the trade was on a scale comparable with that of 1796, before the imposition of Pitt's tax; and there had been no general and maintained development corresponding with the enormously increased demand for horological products.

For better class work, England still maintains a good position, but she is not a serious competitor in the manufacture of the cheapest grades of clocks and watches. High-class watches, ships' chronometers, regulators or astronomical clocks, chiming clocks, and turret clocks are still made in England.

For many years, a few English firms, including

Messrs. Rotherham & Sons, of Coventry, have used automatic machinery for the manufacture of watches; and at the present time there are several factories in this country in which modern automatic machinery is employed for the construction of clocks, the industry having been stimulated by the 33⅓ per cent *ad valorem* duty on imports which was introduced on 29th September 1915. Incidentally, it may be mentioned that the new duty has been more popular among members of the trade than the tax just mentioned, which was imposed by Pitt in 1797. This had such a disastrous effect that it was repealed the following year. It consisted of an annual duty of five shillings for the use of a clock and of ten shillings to half a crown for a watch, the amount varying with the material of which the case was made.

Some idea of the size and variations of the trade can be obtained from the official statistics relating to imports and exports. The tables which follow have been abstracted from the official returns; but corrections, such as for the re-exportation of imports, have not been applied, and inferences as to details should be made with caution.

Table A gives the declared values of imports of clocks and watches separately for the years 1876 to 1890, and also the value of clocks and watches, produced at home, which were exported from the United Kingdom during the same period.

In Table B, particulars are given of the value of exports of home produce for a later period, and separate entries are made for clocks, watches, and parts thereof. It will be noted that the amounts for clocks are now greater than those for watches, but formerly the contrary was the case. In 1870, for example, 80 per cent of the total was for watches.

TRADE 121

TABLE A

Year.	Value of Imports.		Value of Exports.
	Clocks.	Watches.	(*Home Produce only*) Clocks & Watches.
	£	£	£
1876 . . .	446,955	450,067	156,898
1877 . . .	513,387	504,164	154,950
1878 . . .	561,592	512,468	140,890
1879 . . .	543,441	458,588	155,130
1880 . . .	555,018	427,663	156,817
1881 . . .	481,450	467,830	184,123
1882 . . .	526,691	484,192	262,156
1883 . . .	468,664	511,188	311,235
1884 . . .	437,069	606,194	293,039
1885 . . .	408,809	626,482	217,357
1886 . . .	381,265	711,712	207,461
1887 . . .	398,259	750,750	154,459
1888 . . .	469,450	585,587	160,416
1889 . . .	454,556	691,006	139,350
1890 . . .	512,419	674,654	123,127

TABLE B

Value of Exports (*Home Produce only*)

Year.	Clocks.	Parts of Clocks.	Watches.	Parts of Watches.	Total.
	£	£	£	£	£
1908 . . .	22,949	4,545	6,368	5,356	39,218
1909 . . .	26,540	5,107	8,394	2,802	42,843
1910 . . .	30,194	9,139	9,480	9,859	58,672
1911 . . .	33,273	10,425	8,866	6,756	59,320
1912 . . .	35,650	7,682	8,290	6,479	58,101
1913 . . .	36,587	8,727	5,531	6,726	57,571
1914 . . .	26,897	8,450	4,534	10,047	49,928

Table C gives particulars of quantities and values of imports for the three years immediately before the war, with information as to the more important of the exporting countries.

TABLE C

IMPORTS

	Numbers.			Values.		
	1911.	1912.	1913.	1911.	1912.	1913.
Clocks, complete :				£	£	£
From Germany	2,434,152	2,451,555	2,043,866	310,779	335,077	335,902
,, U.S.A.	260,456	422,633	229,470	57,775	74,549	46,672
Total from all countries	2,790,956	2,969,565	2,413,926	417,597	461,832	442,011
Parts of Clocks	—	—	—	44,040	45,367	57,301
Watches, complete:						
With gold cases :						
From Switzerland	137,757	217,636	297,451	233,767	331,611	426,561
Total from all countries.	137,897	218,022	298,480	234,176	332,219	428,066
With silver cases						
From Switzerland	402,062	504,109	658,793	184,195	235,861	297,850
Total from all countries.	406,129	511,118	665,211	185,463	237,918	300,236
With cases of other metals :						
From Switzerland	2,252,855	2,348,853	2,844,223	379,529	400,629	465,197
,, U.S.A.	408,767	303,977	324,283	57,122	43,742	40,061
Total from all countries.	3,052,436	3,002,855	3,535,523	482,464	485,236	546,607
Watch Cases—						
Gold	179,150	270,889	310,916	125,487	168,824	183,972
Silver	443,500	555,781	719,505	45,482	54,951	67,618
Other metals	57,295	84,059	156,662	7,104	12,672	21,449
Parts of Watches other than cases						
From Switzerland				56,192	75,941	82,962
,, U.S.A.				47,587	61,231	106,988
Total from all countries.				114,513	147,375	199,416
Total for Clocks, Watches, and parts thereof				1,656,326	1,946,394	2,246,678

These tables should be taken as evidence of trade rather than manufacture or consumption ; but, with the exception of a few special items, it may be taken that by far the greater part of the imports were for use at home and not for re-exportation. Complete movements without cases are classed as parts, and many foreign watch movements are imported and placed in English-made cases.

TRADE

One of the interesting developments during the war was the appearance of Japan among the more important of the countries from which clocks were imported ; in 1916, the imports from that country included 273,558 clocks of a declared value of £32,152.

The following are the details for the Watch and Clock Trades of the United Kingdom revealed by the Census of Production taken in 1907 for the purpose of obtaining information relating to the output in the various manufactures, and the number of persons engaged in the different workshops and factories which came within the scope of the investigation—

OUTPUT

	No.	Value.
		£
Watches complete—		
With cases of gold	7,500	61,000
,, silver	42,100	59,000
,, other metals	24,400	21,000
'Total watches	74,000	141,000
Watch cases, finished movements, and other parts of watches	—	122,000
Marine chronometers	600	14,000
Turret clocks	—	18,000
Other clocks, complete	41,200	47,000
Clock parts, including movements	—	39,000
Parts of watches and clocks, not separately distinguished	—	19,000
Other products	—	19,000
Total value of goods made	—	419,000
Repairs of Watches, Clocks, and Jewellery	—	185,000
Amount received for work done for the trade	—	9,000
Total value of goods made and work done	—	613,000

124 CLOCKS AND WATCHES

PERSONS EMPLOYED (EXCEPT OUTWORKERS)

	Males.			Females.			Males and Females.		
	Under 18 yrs. of age.	Over 18 yrs. of age.	Total.	Under 18 yrs. of age.	Over 18 yrs. of age.	Total.	Under 18 yrs. of age.	Over 18 yrs. of age.	Total.
Wage-earners	608	2,681	3,289	340	819	1,159	948	3,500	4,448
Salaried persons	23	729	752	25	76	101	48	805	853
Total	631	3,410	4,041	365	895	1,260	996	4,305	5,301

The average number of outworkers in connection with the factories concerned was 302 (286 males and 16 females).

It should be noted that the £185,000 for repairs does not by any means represent the cost of all watch and clock repairs executed in the country; and that retailers with small workshops not engaged in manufacture were not called upon to make returns. This sum of £185,000 is apparently included because it forms part of the output of the workers whose numbers are given.

From the figures, it will be seen that watch and clock-making is not a very important part of British industry; and that, while the exports of home production fell from about £157,000 in 1876 to about £58,000 in 1913, during the same period the imports from abroad increased from about £897,000 to £2,247,000. The decline in the trade is obviously not due to lack of demand for horological products, and serious attempts are being made to restore the industry to a more important position. There have been important developments since 1907, and it may safely be assumed that the present output considerably exceeds the figures recorded in the 1907 census of production returns.

INDEX

AIRY, 39
Alarm clock, 71
Anchor escapement, 29
Apparent solar time, 4
Arnold, 78, 88
Astronomical day, 6

BAIN, 100, 105
Balance spring, 40, 46
Barlow, 68, 92
Barometric error, 37
Board of Longitude, 86
Bracket clock, 96
Breguet, 42, 105
—— spring, 50

CANDLES, 17
Cannon pinion, 55
Caron, 61
Census of Production, 123
Centre-seconds watch, 60
Chronometer, 81, 83, 89
—— escapement, 89
Circular error, 25
Clements, 29
Clepsydrae, 12
Clock cases, 93
—— train, 52
—— -watches, 70
Compensation balance, 78
—— pendulum, 73
Conservatoire des Arts et Métiers, 91
Ctesibius, 14
Cummings, 34
Curb pins, 47, 77
Cylinder escapement, 40

DEAD-BEAT escapement, 31
Declination, 2
Detached escapement, 44, 91
Ditisheim, 82

Domestic clock, 94
Double roller, 46
Duplex escapement, 42
Dutch clocks, 29, 68, 95

EARNSHAW, 79, 89
Einstein, 1
Electric clocks, 99
Electro-magnet, 101
—— -sympathetic clocks, 103
Emperor Charles V, 23
Enamelled cases, 97
Engine turning, 98
English lever, 43, 118
Equation of time, 12
Escapements, 18, 28, 29, 31, 33, 36, 40, 42, 43, 46, 89, 91
Exports, 120

FACCIO, 64
Foliot balance, 18
Forcible correction, 105
Friction wheels, 65
Frisius, 83
Fusee, 22, 56

GALILEO, 25, 27
Gemeente Museum, The Hague, 28
Geneva stop, 58
Gent & Co., 39, 105, 110
Gillett & Johnston, 35
Glastonbury Abbey clock, 19
Graham, 31, 42, 73, 92
Grandfather clock, 95
Gravity escapement, 33
Gridiron pendulum, 74
Grimthorpe, 34
Guillaume, 75, 81

HAIRSPRING, 40, 46
Harris, 27
Harrison, 55, 56, 65, 74, 77, 84

Hele, 21
Hipp's electric clock, 102
Hood clocks, 94
Hooke, 29, 40, 91
Hope-Jones, 108
Horizontal escapement, 40
Hour glass, 16
Huguenin, 63
Huygens, 25, 28

IMPORTS, 120
Impulse dial mechanisms, 100, 109, 112, 115
Invar, 76, 81

JEWELLED bearings, 64
Jones, R. L., 103

KARRUSEL, 51
Kendal, 86
Keyless work, 61
King Alfred, 17

LACQUERED cases, 95
Lantern clock, 94
Le Roy, Julien, 71
Le Roy, Pierre, 78, 81, 91
Lever escapement, 43
Lightfoot, 19
Litherland, 46
Locking plate, 66
Longitude, 83
Loseby, 81
Lund, 105

MAINSPRING, 21
Maintaining power mechanism, 56
Marquetry, 95
Maskelyne, 87, 91
Master clock, 108, 111
Mean solar time, 5
Middle temperature error, 81
Motion work, 55, 59, 60
Movement-making, 117
Mudge, 34, 43, 46, 65, 86

NEWTON, 1
Nuremberg eggs, 97

OIL clocks, 17

PENDULUM, 25
—— suspension, 35
Pinchbeck, 98
Pitt's tax, 120
Pond's electric clock, 102
Prescot, 117
Prest, 62
Primitive methods, 10
Production census, 123
" Pulsynetic " system, 110

QUARE, 71

RACK lever escapement, 46
—— striking mechanism, 68
Radium " clock," 115
—— dials, 116
Reclûs, 110
Recoil escapement, 29
" Reflex " pendulum control, 105
Regulation, 36, 47
Relativity, 1
Remontoire, 33
Repeaters, 70
Repoussé work, 97
Riefler escapement, 36
Right ascension, 3
Ritchie & Son, 103, 105
Rotherham & Sons, 120
Royal pendulum, 94

SAND glass, 16
Science Museum, 20, 27, 65, 87
Secondary temperature compensation, 81
Self-Winding Clock Co., 102
Self-winding watches, 61
Sheep's-head clocks, 94
Sidereal time, 3
Silent Electric Co., 115
Stackfreed, 22
Standard time, 5
Stop watches, 60
—— work, 57, 58
Striking mechanisms, 66
Sully, 65

Sun dial, 11
Synchronome Co., 108

TABLE clocks, 93
Temperature compensation, 73
Thornbridge transmitter, 113
Time, 1
Tompion, 41, 91
Tourbillon, 50
Trades, 118
Transmitter, 108, 111

VERGE escapement, 18
Vick, 21

Victoria and Albert Museum, 97
Vulliamy, 65

" WAITING TRAIN " movement, 113
Watch cases, 96
—— train, 56
Water clocks, 12
Westminster clock, 34, 37
Wireless time signals, 115
Wycherly, 117

YEAR, 7

ZECH, 22

www.ingramcontent.com/pod-product-compliance
Lightning Source LLC
Chambersburg PA
CBHW030117170426
43198CB00009B/651